Walking on Water

Walking on Water

DAVE CARLEY

Signature
EDITIONS

Cover design by Terry Gallagher/Doowah Design.
Cover painting by JoEllen Brydon.
Photograph of Dave Carley by Michael Lee.
Published with the assistance of The Canada Council for the Arts.
Printed and bound in Canada by AGMV Marquis Imprimeur.

Canadian Cataloguing in Publication Data

Carley, Dave, 1955–
Walking on Water

(Performance Series)
A play.
ISBN 0-921833-72-5

I. Title. II. Series: Performance series (Winnipeg, Man.)

PS8555.A7397W34 2000 C812'. 54 C00-901389-X
PR9199.3.C337W34 2000

Signature Editions, P.O. Box 206, RPO Corydon, Winnipeg, MB, R3M 3S7

For Margaret Carley

Walking on Water premiered at Prairie Theatre Exchange, Winnipeg, on March 30, 2000, with the following cast:

Heck Munro—Tom Anniko
Betty Warner—Sharon Bajer
Chalmers Wilkie—Brian Drader
Max Bloom—Darcy Fehr
Sadie Munro—Martine Friesen
Lee Kwan—Oscar Hsu
Jean Findlay Copeland—Patricia Hunter
Archie Copeland—Stan Lesk
Terry Andrews—Carson Nattrass
Chief Percy Bromell—Harry Nelken
Neil Griffin—Jason Neufeld
Christine MacCosham—Anne Ross
Reverend Land—David Warburton

Director—Allen MacInnes
Set and Costume Design—Craig Sandells
Lighting Design—Scott Henderson
Sound Composer—Greg Lowe
Voice Coach—Sheila Langston
Movement Coach—Bryan Doubt
Stage Manager—Maureen Shelley
Assistant Stage Manager—Marlene Meaden
PTE General Manager—Cherry Karpyshin

Walking on Water was next presented by New Stages Peterborough at Showplace Peterborough, in August, 2000, with the following cast and crew:

Heck Munro—Jack Roe
Betty Warner—Leah Baric
Chalmers Wilkie—Mark Brownell
Max Bloom—Phil Oakley
Sadie Munro—Marjorie Wingrove
Lee Kwan—Oscar Hsu
Jean Findlay Copeland—Dianne Latchford
Archie Copeland—Chuck Vollmar
Terry Andrews—Vince Bruni
Chief Percy Bromell—Syd Waldron
Neil Griffin—Darren Keay
Christine MacCosham—Katie O'Rourke
Reverend Land—James Kirchner

Director—Michael Waller
Set Design— Al Tye
Costume Design—Jennifer Triemstra
Lighting Design—Peter Freund
Sound Design—David Moes
Stage Manager—Stephen Souter
Assistant Stage Managers—Sandy Plunkett and Sara Tye
Technical Director—Don White
Props—Pauline Siddall

Characters

(age as of 1949)

Neil Griffin. 22. Reporter for *The Ashburnham Gazette*. Christine's boyfriend.

Christine MacCosham. 19. Student. Neil's girlfriend.

Sadie Munro. 39. Married to Heck.

Heck Munro. 45. Married to Sadie. Editor/Owner of *The Ashburnham Gazette*.

Lee Kwan. Early 30s. Munro family chauffeur.

Betty Warner. 30. Heck Munro's mistress. Terry's sister.

Terry Andrews. 25. Felon. Betty's brother.

Archie Copeland. 40. Husband of Jean Findlay Copeland.

Jean Findlay Copeland. 40. Wife of Archie.

Reverend Wilfrid Land. 60. Presbyterian minister.

Max Bloom. Early 30s. Owner of Bloom's Furniture. No accent.

Chief Percy Bromell. 55. Police chief.

Chalmers Wilkie. 50. Undertaker.

Locale

In and around Ashburnham, a city of 50,000 in 1949, growing to 250,000 by the end of the century.

Act I—Water Street
Act II—The Ashburnham Necropolis

Notes

There is no built set.

The playing of the piece should be seamless and devoid of scene breaks.

Where I have ended a character's speech with (a few bracketed words), my intent is that the subsequent character begins his or her speech over those words.

The characters don't "age."

Max Bloom has no accent.

"Ash-burn-um." The first two syllables are equally stressed; the last is not.

Neil speaks frequently to the audience. I have not marked those direct addresses, unless I felt that the focus of Neil's speech was not immediately clear. I have marked all of the other characters' speeches to the audience.

I have described props and indicated their usage, but they are not essential and, for the sake of thematic simplicity, directors may wish to dispense with both props and multiple costumes.

Max Bloom's quote on page 58 is from F.D. Hemans (1793-1835) "The Child's First Grief."

And, finally, the disclaimer: This is a work of fiction. None of the characters is based on anyone alive, dead or related.

Act One

Music.

Stage is empty, black.

Characters emerge in half light and move towards the audience. LEE *stands apart from the others.*

ALL: *(Murmuring, not together, virtually inaudible.)* We are the dead. We are the dead… (Etc.)

Rising sound of bulldozers; disquiet among the dead; some rhubarb; they begin dispersing. Black.

Dawn searing across the back of the open stage. Old alarm clock. Another alarm. Fifty thousand alarms of varying degrees and intensity. Alarms banged out. Light up on NEIL.

NEIL: Sorry about the alarms. It used to just take three. But there's less incentive to get up—now that I'm dead. Except today. I mean, tonight. *(Or, "this afternoon.")* Right now, we've got nothing but incentive. I'm going to solve a murder. Not mine. His.

NEIL *gestures over to* LEE, *who is lounging on a tombstone—likely a chair.*

Trust me: As soon as we know who killed him, we'll have solved all the mysteries of the universe. At least our little corner of it. And once we have that knowledge, we'll be redeemed, as if the sun burned off the anonymous mist that (enshrouds our souls)

HECK: Get started! They don't need the fancy stuff.

NEIL: So you just sit there, and imagine it's—what?—6:04 in the A.M. on Friday, June 17. 1949. And you're looking down on my city, Ashburnham. *(So HECK can't hear.)* As if you're turning pages in the novel I never got to finish. As if my novel had pictures.

Rising sound of bulldozer interrupts; heavy machinery and beeping. Bulldozer sound dies out.

I don't know exactly where you could stand in Ashburnham to have such a clear vantage point. Of us. Of our story. There's a hill on the east side, rising like a verdant, pustulent boil. *(Speaking over a derisive response from some of the others.)* OK, OK—there's a big green hill. I'm just being creative.

HECK: There's not enough time.

CHIEF: Let the lad talk.

CHRISTINE: Yes, let him. Go on, honey.

NEIL: You probably know Ashburnham, or some reasonable facsimile. We like to think we're unique but, really, we're like any place anywhere, maybe prettier because of the hill, and the river there, curling through town like a—like a life-flushing intestine. *(Ignoring a few jeers.)* We invent things here: breakfast cereal, fibreglass fishing boats, uh, well, that's two.

CHRISTINE: Disposable pens!

WILKIE: Fabulous new trends in mortuary procedure!

NEIL: We've got a university, a normal school for teachers—

HECK: And, for those who didn't make it into either, there's the Bible college.

LAND: *(Good-naturedly.)* You'll rot in hell for that!

NEIL: We've got factories making boats and motors and over there the mill is puffing the wheat we're going to box and ship all over North America—our cereal will be getting soggy next week in some California bowl. *(Sees that HECK et al. are getting impatient.)* We should get started.

Sounds of assent from the others.

June, 1949. Behind you, to the east—the first spears of dawn— *(Notices that dawn is actually spreading behind him.)* That's not right—why's it back there?

HECK: Because that's the way they're facing. Give them your byline, Kid.

NEIL: Aw, did I forget? I'm Neil, Neil Griffin, I'm with *The Gazette*. Criminal court beat, city council beat. Hey—there's a difference?

WILKIE: That was cynical.

LAND: You died too young to be cynical.

NEIL: *(Confessional.)* I'll tell you my dirty secret.

LAND: It's hardly a secret.

NEIL: I'm working on a novel.

HECK: A purple string of adjectives and (adverbs)

CHRISTINE: It would've been a good one!

SADIE: We'll never know, will we?

NEIL: You're not supposed to talk about being a writer, because talking kills the doing. But it's important you know I can look beyond mere facts and statistics and see the, uh, grey rain battering the pavement as Dorothy lies bleeding to death.

Some groans.

HECK: Who the hell's Dorothy? I've been wondering who this Dorothy was ever since I read (that thing on your desk)

Bulldozers again, rising above HECK's preceding. LEE comes out to the garage. He flicks the light on. Bulldozers cut out.

NEIL: He's not wasting any time. Day one. 6:15 A.M. That's Lee, the Munros' driver. Lee, uh… I can't remember his last name. Sorry. It's short. Damn. Why is that? I can remember Bassingthwaite—

SADIE: *(Under.)* (Kwan)

NEIL: —or Winslow-Cochrane—

SADIE: (Kwan!)

NEIL: —but I cannot remember Lee *(Tries.)* Lee, uh.

SADIE: Kwan!

NEIL: Kwan! Kwan. Kwan.

LEE is whistling.

He won't be happy for long. That car's his nemesis. It's a '38 Packard. Why, you ask, does Heck Munro have an eleven-year-old car when he's one of the richest men in town?

ARCHIE: *(Miserably.)* "Ask the man who owns one."

Sound of failed ignition, under.

CHIEF: *(Snorts.)* Ask the stuck-up arsehole.

HECK: I won it.

LEE is swearing in Cantonese.

NEIL: Just don't ask the poor sucker who can't get it started on a damp June morning.

More swearing from LEE.

We'll leave Lee—Lee, damn—Lee KWAN—let's leave him to his automotive hell.

SADIE *appears.*

SADIE: Heck? Where are you?

NEIL: Whoah—we just jumped forty-five minutes. That's Sadie Munro, my boss's wife—she's still alive—and now it's 7:00 A.M.

SADIE: Heck! Heck! I want the car today—I thought Lee and I would go up to the island and—Heck?

Sound of door slapping shut offstage.

Typical: he didn't hear a word I said.

NEIL: *(Consulting watch.)* It's exactly 7:00 A.M.

SADIE: We already know that.

NEIL: It doesn't hurt to repeat—it'll be important later.

SADIE: Not as important as you think. *(To Audience.)* 7:01 now.

NEIL: "Not as important—" What did she mean by that?

7:01 A.M. Same slapping door sound. HECK *appears in the garage.* LEE*'s legs are sticking out.*

HECK: On the fritz again? *(Laughs.)* Someday I'm going to buy you a Caddy. A brand new Caddy. You want a Caddy, Lee? I'll walk to work. If anything comes over the wire I'll have The Kid bring it to you.

HECK *leaves.*

NEIL: I'm "The Kid." Mr. Munro's the editor and owner of *The Gazette* and the wires are buzzing—the

Communists have just shanghai'd Shanghai. Mr. Munro's fascinated by China and it turns out Lee has a certain, special interest too. So Mr. Munro lets him know when anything significant comes over the wire. He also makes me take over the baseball scores—Lee runs a pool with the Chinamen. Baseball, not hockey. Mr. Munro draws the line at hockey. He says baseball is eugenically superior to hockey.

HECK: Hockey should only be played in caves.

NEIL: He wrote an editorial last April Fool's (Day saying)

HECK: "Thirty-two percent of all NHL forwards are skating on three toes." *(To Audience.)* Half the fool city believed me!

ARCHIE: That's it! I've had enough!

NEIL: We got to get over to the bridge!

ARCHIE is on the bridge.

That's Archie Copeland, he's at the Water Street bridge—again—and he's planning to jump. Again.

ARCHIE: I can't go on.

NEIL: Arch, Arch…

ARCHIE: Well, I can't. This world is absurdly cruel.

NEIL: Yeah, yeah.

ARCHIE: *(Grabbing at NEIL's arm.)* I'm going through with it this time!

NEIL: *(Not serious.)* Oh, please don't jump, Arch. *(To Audience.)* He never will. Jump. At least (intentionally.)

ARCHIE: Here I go!

NEIL: *(Still not serious.)* Think of your wife.

ARCHIE: That's exactly what I'm doing.

NEIL: *(To Audience.)* The trouble is—well, I'll let Archie tell you the problem:

ARCHIE: *(Hesitating.)* D'you think it's high enough?

NEIL: *(To Audience.)* It's 1949—the city's still horizontal.

ARCHIE: What do you think?

NEIL: Not if you want to be a hundred percent sure.

ARCHIE: Goddamn this city!

NEIL: So what's it going to be?

ARCHIE collects himself and walks off.

ARCHIE: *(Exiting.)* I'll find a higher bridge, even if I have to go to—to Niagara Falls. Yeah, I'll try the one at Niagara Falls—

BETTY Warner becomes visible, surveying Water Street.

NEIL: *(Hurrying.)* 7:20. I try to be at my desk before Mr. Munro arrives. I'm actually working on my novel—but he thinks I'm as eager as he is to see what happened in the world while we slept. *(Confides.)* I need a raise; I'm getting married... *(Distracted by BETTY by now.)* Not to her! She lives across Water Street from *The Gazette*, in the apartments. She's new to town, and no one's quite sure where she's from. You're thinking: "There's fifty thousand of you; how do you know someone's new?" Well, if twenty reporters at *The Gazette* don't recognize her, she's new.

A quick story before Mr. Munro gets here. It's something I learned in the future—but actually it happened back in January. It was 10 P.M., and Mr. Munro was just leaving the office and thinking about either a) going for a drink at the Empress or b) less palatable, going home to Sadie.

HECK: a).

NEIL: He turned the corner on to Water and there she was.

BETTY is fumbling with keys.

Mr. Munro, being a gentleman, especially when it's ten at night and he doesn't want to go home—

HECK: Let me hold your bags.

BETTY: I can manage.

HECK watches, amused, as BETTY struggles.

HECK: You're new in town.

BETTY: Says who?

HECK: Says I.

BETTY: Who are you to decide who's new?

HECK: I'm Heck Munro. *(Nods across street.)* I own *The Gazette*. And you?

BETTY: I'm the Crown Princess of Albania.

HECK: That so?

BETTY: Zig. Daughter of Zog.

HECK: *(Laughs.)* OK, Zig. Ask me something in Albanian.

BETTY: *(Indicating her apartment.)* Vodka or whiskey, comrade?

NEIL: And that was that. Zig Zag Zog. But I didn't figure out about Mr. Munro and her for a long time.

ARCHIE: You're too naive to be a novelist.

HECK: Don't distract him, Arch.

BETTY: I thought you were looking for a bridge.

ARCHIE: First I'm gonna check the steeple of First Presbyterian—maybe I can shinny up it—

NEIL: I especially should've guessed about Mr. Munro and Betty after this particular morning because this is what I saw at 7:30 A.M.—note the time: it's now 7:30.

NEIL points over to BETTY, who is looking out her window. She blows a kiss down at HECK.

And one minute later, Simon Legree's arrived—

HECK: *(Entering, whistling.)* Morning, Kid. First here again?

NEIL: Yes, sir.

HECK: You remind me of me. *(Beat.)* Take that as a compliment.

NEIL: Compliment taken, sir.

HECK has idly picked up a piece of paper on NEIL's desk; NEIL is horrified.

HECK: Anything come over the wire?

NEIL: Princess Elizabeth is in Scotland.

HECK: *(Snort of derision, then reads paper.)* "Dorothy was lying on the pocked pavement in the grey rain"?

NEIL: Oh, that's a, uh—

HECK: Too many adjectives, Kid. Adjectives are subjective.

NEIL: *(Retrieving paper.)* Adjectives are (subjective, yessir)

HECK: And this Dorothy. She have a last name? Miss or Mrs? Speaking of which: heard a rumour you're getting married.

NEIL: *(To Audience.)* We hadn't told a soul. (Who told him?)

HECK: When?

NEIL: September, sir.

HECK: Well, make sure the little missus continues to get you here this early.

HECK starts to exit, turns.

I expect you'll be wanting a raise. Talk to me in August.

HECK leaves. NEIL makes triumphant sign, then remembers.

NEIL: Shoot, I'll be dead by then. Actually, one person did know Christine and I were getting hitched—her minister, Reverend Land.

LAND becomes visible. He's dialling, but he covers the receiver.

LAND: I might have accidentally conveyed uh your joyous news. Now, if you'll excuse me, I'm ringing Sadie Munro—

NEIL: Give her time for a coffee.

LAND hangs up.

It'll turn out that Land's pretty indiscreet in a pivotal way, but we don't know that yet. And you'll meet my fiancée, Christine, shortly, but first let me reintroduce you to Sadie Munro—you didn't get a very good impression of her earlier.

Light up on SADIE.

She never comes to *The Gazette*—that's her husband's domain. But everyone knows her. She's energetically sad. By that, I mean her sadness has come to envelope the city like a blanket of (comforting down)

There are a few throat clearings from the others.

Is this the morning ritual of a well-adjusted person?

SADIE: *(Reading obituaries.)* "Hilary Jenkins, 83, at peace with the Lord, after a valiant seven-year battle."

NEIL: She's got nothing to be sad about. She's as rich as anyone gets in Ashburnham, Mr. Munro doesn't interfere with her life, she's 39—that's old, (sure, but)

SADIE: It's older than you'll ever be. You tragic child. *(Reading.)* "Avery Tedford, 75." What a dog's life he had.

NEIL: Her life consists of driving up Water Street to where it becomes Highway 28, and from there going north thirty-five miles to her island on Lake Kawartha. She collects wildflowers. Then she returns, back down Water, right through town to the Necropolis, where she decorates graves.

SADIE: *(To Audience.)* I love the dead. I give them respect, they give me joy.

ARCHIE is sneaking into his house.

NEIL: Archie's decided to live another day.

JEAN: *(To Audience.)* This may not be in his hands.

ARCHIE runs into JEAN.

Just getting home, are we?

ARCHIE: No.

JEAN: You were at Bloom's.

ARCHIE: No.

JEAN smacks him.

I wasn't!

JEAN smacks him again.

JEAN: You were!

ARCHIE: Was not!

JEAN smacks him again.

OK, I was.

JEAN turns to Audience and shrugs: "That was easy."

JEAN: *(Back to ARCHIE.)* How much was it this time? HOW MUCH! Five hundred! A thousand?

ARCHIE: The cottage.

JEAN: GODDAMN YOU!

JEAN launches herself at ARCHIE and unleashes a storm of blows on him, which he takes passively. This continues, under the following.

NEIL: That's Jean, Archie's husband, and that's how she starts her day, oh, about once a week. Did I call her Archie's husband?

JEAN: *(Stops hitting ARCHIE; to NEIL.)* Sure. Make a joke.

NEIL: It's just that—well, (look at you)

JEAN: Oh, I know. You see that pathetic thing on the bridge, doing his "Will I, won't I jump?" and you think, "Who—could be driving him to this?" And your dull little reporter brain says, "Cherchez the wife." Well Mr. Would-be Novelist, why do you think I start my day like this "Oh, about once a week"? WHY! Because he just lost my island! And before that he lost my car, my paintings (my silver, my Crown Derby, my)

NEIL: We should keep this thing (going)

HECK: Get back to (the story)

ARCHIE: Yes, please, I have my one good line coming up.

JEAN: Get out!

ARCHIE: I'll never go to Bloom's again, I swear!

JEAN: Swear on what! Swear on my money!? Get out, Archie! Get out and don't come back! GET OUT! *(Pause.)* Why are you standing there?

ARCHIE: If I go, what will you have left?

LAND: *(Checks watch.)* 8:25. Time for me to start opening my big mouth?

NEIL: Please.

Phone rings. Light up on SADIE at one end of stage, picking up phone.

SADIE: Riverside 20189. *(Two-oh-one-eight-nine.)*

LAND: Sadie—it's Wilf Land.

SADIE: This is early, Reverend. Has someone died? Let me guess: it's Alpha Burgess. She's finally crossed over. I'm going up north to get flowers; I'll get some (for Alpha)

LAND: Alpha's made a rally. No—it's something else. I've an odd request. Your driver Lee was here yesterday and he told me something. It kept me up all night...

NEIL muzzles LAND's phone.

Why'd you do that!

NEIL: I don't want them to hear the "odd request" yet.

LAND: Why not!

NEIL: Dramatic structure.

LAND mouths "dramatic structure?" to Audience.

(To Audience.) I am, after all, the omniscient narrator, the story God.

LAND: Story God? That's a bit offensive.

JEAN: Someone's getting big for his britches.

TERRY: You want me to take him down now?

LAND: If you won't let me blab, at least introduce me properly.

NEIL: OK—Sadie Munro's minister. Wilfrid Land: The Indiscreet Presbyterian.

LAND: Indiscreet—not in the sexual sense.

HECK: Indiscreet as in a big mouth.

LAND: It's true. It's my cross. I have a huge, flapping trap.

NEIL: Land's church is also on Water Street. You're going to think nothing happens anywhere else in this town and, for the purpose of this story, it doesn't. But if you're expecting Land to be one of those dour Calvinists, think again. He's—how to describe him?

HECK: *(To Audience.)* Theological tapioca.

NEIL: OK, resume your conversation. Just the last bit.

LAND: —So, as you can see, I didn't want to do anything before getting your say-so.

SADIE: Yes, of course. Full steam ahead. Thank you, Reverend.

SADIE puts the phone down and gives herself over to a wail of agony and anger.

NEIL: That—is not "energetically sad" you're witnessing. That is energetically something else. *(Consulting watch.)* 8:29 A.M. I hope you're remembering these times.

BETTY: Oh yeah, they're all taking notes.

Sound of bulldozers.

HECK: How close are they?

NEIL: I've still got time.

Lights up on BLOOM and CHIEF, both asleep.

Ah—Ashburnham's sleeping beauties. That one, that's Max Bloom, owner of Bloom's Furniture.

BLOOM: *(Sits up and goes into spiel.)* This chair—if you're wondering, is it Danish? Well, you'd be right. It's Danish and, boy, is it comfy. Perfect for your family room. Did I say family? I'm a family man, too. I've got the two finest boys, wait a sec. *(Produces snapshots.)* Ron and Jay—

HECK: No time, Max.

BLOOM: They can pass them around while we talk.

HECK: No.

NEIL: Anyway, you're supposed to be unconscious.

BLOOM: You two got something against children?

HECK: We've got something against wasting time.

NEIL: Pin them up in the lobby at intermission.

BLOOM: Can I at least tell them about my house? *(Before NEIL can stop him; to Audience.)* We just built in the west end: a four bedroom ranch-style, acres of glass and—no basement!

BETTY: Imagine—a house with no basement.

LAND: Seems perverse. Like heaven with no hell.

BETTY: Yeah, heaven with no hell. That's real perverse.

NEIL: *(Returns BLOOM to his sleeping position on the couch.)* Here's where you have to watch your first impression. It might look like Bloom's waking up with a hangover. Also, he's on a chair with a price tag, which suggests he spent the night at his store.

BLOOM: *(Coming to.)* Oh, my head. (What happened?)

NEIL: The obvious inference is that Archie Copeland isn't the only one in trouble with the missus. But not going home, that's not in character. Bloom often works late, but he's madly in love with his wife and, anyway, he doesn't drink.

Bloom begins stumbling off.

Yeah, get yourself home, Max.

NEIL indicates a huge, sleeping mound.

CHIEF: *(In his sleep.)* Sunny-side up.

NEIL: The other sleeping beauty is our police chief, Percy Bromell.

CHIEF: *(In his sleep.)* Blueberry pancakes.

NEIL: He's dreaming of the morning imperative.

CHIEF: *(Waking.)* Breakfast. Syrup. Johnnycake. Flapjacks. Syrup. Maple syrup. Brown sugar.

NEIL: Take another five, Chief.

CHIEF: Thanks, Scoop.

Chalmers WILKIE is enjoying a cigarette, having just finished Avery Tedford. He will periodically touch up the corpse.

NEIL: Chalmers Wilkie is our leading mortician. He's finishing up Avery Tedford, who died of old age and overwork two days ago. Tedford was a farmer but Wilkie's powdered him up like he never saw a minute of sun.

WILKIE: That's not true! They'll say, "He looks like he's having a nap under the elm tree." *(To Audience, over snickers.)* I'm an artist. I believe in the transformative power of my profession.

NEIL: Which is just as well, because tonight Sadie Munro's going to bring you your greatest challenge. *(To Audience again.)* She's going to bring Wilkie a corpse that will at first fill him with terror, but which he will come to regard as a pivotal step in his own career. The corpse Sadie's bringing will be Wilkie's second epiphany in one day. The first is going to happen—right—about—now:

WILKIE puts the final dab of lipstick on the corpse. He regards the lipstick for a moment. He brings the lipstick up to his own lips, pauses, then applies.

WILKIE: Oh. Ahhh. Oooh.

NEIL: Never, never kiss an undertaker.

CHRISTINE appears, carrying books.

I gotta show you my girl.

CHRISTINE: *(To Audience.)* "My girl"?

NEIL: Christine was born the day the stock market crashed. Her dad took that as an omen, hit the rails and was never seen again. But Christine and her mom toughed it out and now she's at normal school.

CHRISTINE: Teachers' college! (Honestly, Neil)

NEIL: Three nights a week she cleans Bloom's store and, well, I go over there and help her finish up and then we, uh, test the furniture. The beds—(you know)

CHRISTINE: You don't have to tell them everything!

NEIL's phone rings. He answers.

NEIL: Newsroom. Griffin.

CHRISTINE: *(Conspiratorial.)* It's "your girl." I'm phoning from the corner.

NEIL: Oh, honey doll.

CHRISTINE: I think you should come down here.

NEIL: But Mr. Munro—

CHRISTINE: I got something pretty nice I want to whisper in your ear.

NEIL has a horny fit. He hangs up and runs out of the newsroom, past HECK.

NEIL: *(Leaving.)* Another purse snatching, sir!

HECK: So much for our reliable narrator. Crazy kid. Has he introduced everyone?

Light has come up on TERRY, who's punching a bag at the YMCA.

TERRY: Not me.

TERRY stops, awaiting recognition.

HECK: Your type hardly needs introducing.

TERRY: Pardon me; my "type"?

HECK: You heard me.

TERRY: What do you know about my type?

NEIL has arrived on the street and tries to talk to CHRISTINE, only to be interrupted repeatedly by TERRY's catalogue of woe.

(To Audience.) As it turns out, sixty percent of my "type" have learning handicaps. Dyslexia. Attention Deficit Disorder. Not to mention broken homes. Socio-economic dysfunction. My "type"? We're victims.

NEIL: Are you done?

TERRY: Be my guest.

NEIL: I've got to go back up before Mr. Munro notices I'm gone.

CHRISTINE: I missed you last night. Three ways.

NEIL groans.

Do you want to know the three ways?

NEIL: Yes, yes and yes!

CHRISTINE: Mr. Bloom's got in three new Sealy Posturepedics with individual coil support. They're like trampolines. If we don't hurry up and try them out someone's going to buy them. Untested. You said you'd stop 'round.

NEIL: Council went to 11:00 and I couldn't leave.

CHRISTINE: That's OK. Maybe they'll be there tonight. Maybe not. Darn. I don't work again till tomorrow. But never mind about that—I have to tell you something else ultra-amazing!

HECK clears throat.

NEIL: It'll have to wait. Mr. Munro hates his reporters wasting time.

CHRISTINE: But it's going to change our lives!

NEIL: If he fires me it'll really change our lives.

CHRISTINE: Neil!

NEIL: I'll pick you up at nine. We'll drive up the river.

CHRISTINE: Neil! Come back here!

NEIL exits quickly. CHRISTINE shakes her fist at his retreating figure, and moves off.

NEIL: Is there no God! That I should be taken before I could try out those mattresses.

TERRY has resumed punching the bag.

And all because of that bastard! His name's Terry Andrews. Recognize the "type"?

TERRY: There's that word again!

NEIL: Every self-respecting city has a handful—the habitual felon, perpetually in a state of just coming out or going back in prison. He's been back here for about a year now, after doing some time for armed robbery. He held up the Royal Bank in Madoc.

TERRY: Cruddy two-bit craphole! I shoulda got away with it.

NEIL: And he might've—except it was August and the balaclava he was wearing was wool.

TERRY: I'm itching, so I gotta take it off!

HECK: So he goes barefaced and then, when he runs out of the bank, twenty thousand in hand—

NEIL: Snap, crackle, pop, cheese!

TERRY: Stupid town's fulla tourists and one's takin' a picture of the scenic bank!

CHIEF: Which kinda sealed the evidence requirement.

HECK: What a front page that was.

CHIEF: He still mighta got away except that just outside of town he did something real stupid—

TERRY: Should never'a stopped for a smoke.

CHIEF: *(With gun.)* Gotcha!

HECK: So Terry went to Kingston, where he cooled his heels for three years and now I've got just one question to ask of the judicial process. Editorial: "Why do we let convicts lift weights?"

NEIL: That's right! We should force-feed them cake and mashed potatoes! If he wasn't so goddamn strong I might've had sex with Christine twenty thousand more times by now! I wouldn't be spending eternity with blueballs!

Pause. Everyone looks embarrassed.

HECK: I think, in the interests of brevity, we can skip over the discussion of your gonads.

NEIL: Sorry, sir.

CHRISTINE: In the interests of my reputation, too.

NEIL: Sure. So. So, that's my city. I mean, that's a sample. There's fifty thousand others out there living on a hundred and forty streets, but it's just this bunch and what they're going to do on Water that matters to us tonight. *(Or "this afternoon.")*

NEIL checks his watch. He's expecting something. Then: light up on SADIE Munro.

Right on time.

SADIE: Where are you!

NEIL: *(Pointing up the time for Audience.)* It's 8:30.

SADIE: Lee—where are you? Lee!

SADIE arrives in garage. LEE's legs are sticking out from under the Packard and she doesn't see them at first.

Where are you! WHERE ARE YOU! Oh, there you are. COME OUT OF THERE AND TALK TO ME!

SADIE kicks LEE's feet.

COME OUT OF THERE!

NEIL switches the garage light off and moves forward, in front of SADIE.

NEIL: At this point, the novelist in me—ever conscious of structure—intervenes again.

A buzzer. Light up on HECK.

Yes, sir—you wanted me?

HECK: *(Very affable.)* Kid, what do you know about China?

NEIL: Not much until you write about it, sir.

HECK: *(To Audience.)* Smarmy bugger. *(To NEIL.)* It's clear the Nationalists have lost to Mao. Think that's a bad thing? *(Doesn't wait for answer.)* I don't. The Nationalists are corrupt and Mao seems to be the genuine article. 'Course I can't say that too loudly, can I? *(Doesn't wait for answer.)* Mao's a Commie. But either we go with Mao or he goes with someone else, and you know who he'll choose.

NEIL: The Russians.

HECK: Exactly. Which leaves who as beacons of the free world?

NEIL: *(He's heard this before.)* Witless Yanks.

HECK: And—dickless Brits. I'm going to write a series of essays, put 'em on the wire, and while I'm writing this international perspective you'll do something local; glad you volunteered. I want a parallel feature on the Chinamen of Ashburnham. Who they are, when they came here, what they think of Mao Zedong. You can begin with my driver, Lee. You met him?

NEIL: When I take the baseball (scores over)

HECK: He's the easiest to start with—his old man brought him here when he was a tadpole and his English is better than mine. Less purple than yours. Give him a call today, set it up. He and Sadie are probably going up to the lake this morning, but they'll be back later.

Phone rings.

Get that.

NEIL: *The Gazette*. Mr. Munro's office. Oh—Mrs. Munro, just a moment.

HECK indicates he doesn't want to talk to her.

Sorry ma'am. He's just gone into a meeting. Can he—oh. Oh. That's terrible, Mrs. Munro. I'll tell him right away.

NEIL hangs up.

(To Audience.) Mr. Munro once told me:

HECK: *(To NEIL.)* A good journalist is never fooled by coincidence. Novelists use coincidence all the time. Novelists are weaklings.

NEIL: *(To Audience.)* So explain that call I just took, coming exactly when I was being asked by Mr. Munro to go interview Lee.

HECK: What's she want?

NEIL: She says your driver, Lee—he's dead.

HECK: What's that?

NEIL: He's dead.

HECK: You're joking.

NEIL: No, sir, I wouldn't joke about (something like that)

HECK: Lee's dead?

NEIL: Yes sir. That's what Mrs. Munro said, she just found him.

HECK: But I talked to him a couple of hours ago. I was just telling you to go interview him.

NEIL: Coincidence, eh? *(Quick.)* Mrs. Munro says to come right over.

HECK: I don't have my car—you have yours, Kid?

NEIL: I drove him the seven blocks up Water to their house. It's a red brick pile girdled with striped awnings—looks like it's squatting, knees bent, wanting to flap the hell out of town. Mrs. Munro was standing by the garage. *(Checks watch, for Audience's benefit.)* 9:15.

HECK: You're sure he's dead.

SADIE: Of course I'm sure.

HECK: He was alive when I left this morning.

SADIE: Well, he's dead now. He's in there.

HECK: Who've you called?

SADIE: No one. Hello, Neil.

NEIL: I'm very (sorry, Mrs. Munro)

HECK: What happened?

SADIE: I went out to the garage.

HECK: When?

SADIE: I don't know. 8:30. He was under the car.

HECK: Well, I suppose we'd best take a look.

Light up on LEE, lying beside the car.

Thought you said he was underneath.

SADIE: I pulled him out. When he didn't—I could tell right away he was—I couldn't leave him under there!

HECK: Poor devil must've had a heart attack or (a seizure or)

NEIL: Sir, he's had a bang. *(Points out abrasion.)*

SADIE is feeling her ear. An earring is missing. NEIL notices.

SADIE: Maybe when I pulled him out.

HECK looks long and hard at SADIE.

HECK: Kid, go find Chief Bromell. Try the Coffee Shop at the Y. He's not going to like being disturbed, so make sure he knows it's me who wants him. Get him here fast. And don't tell anyone else.

Light up on CHIEF, who is scarfing back breakfast and addressing the Coffee Shop. At the other end of the counter, TERRY watches him. NEIL arrives.

CHIEF: ...So Branch Rickey has three Negroes: Robinson, Roy Campanella and that new lad, whatsit. That's fine and good; the Dodgers've got home run capability now so Heck writes this editorial, says this proves the value of integration 'cause the Dodgers, the only integrated team in the league, are going to win the pennant.

NEIL: (Sir?)

CHIEF: And that's fine and good and by God I stand four-square for integration—weren't so long ago they wouldn't let an Irish Catholic like me on the force. But Heck hasn't thunk it through.

NEIL: (Sir)

CHIEF: What does it say about integration if the Dodgers get all the way to the World Series—and them all-white Yankees whup their asses—again?

NEIL: Sir?

CHIEF: Can't you see I'm eating breakfast?

NEIL: My boss sent me (to get you)

CHIEF: I'm a mind-reader. Let me guess. Your boss is J. Edgar Hoover and you're come to tell me John Dillinger's escaped from hell.

Mirth from others, including TERRY.

Look—I even made the jailbird laugh.

NEIL: My boss is Heck Munro.

CHIEF: Now you look familiar. You're the cub reporter who's been making police court sound like a B movie. What does His Nibs want?

NEIL: He's got a dead man in his garage.

CHIEF: There he goes again—talking like the movies.

NEIL: But it's true, sir.

CHIEF: Well, can the dead man wait till after I've had my pancakes?

NEIL: The dead man can, but I doubt Mr. Munro will.

CHIEF: *(Sighs and gets up.)* No, I suppose not.

NEIL: *(To Audience.)* When you're planning on being a novelist you spend a lot of time observing the little things.

Light on CHIEF, who has begun moving.

Like the way a big man like Percy Bromell slides off his stool and glides, as imperceptibly as a glacier, out of the Y Coffee Shop—and on to the case.

Light on TERRY.

Or like the tattoo on the bicep of the felon who's sneering down the counter at you.

Light up on SADIE *feeling earlobe.*

Or like the expression on a woman's face when she can't find an earring and knows she'd better—and then she spots it.

SADIE *puts foot over earring.*

CHIEF: Looks like he's had a crack or two on the noggin.

SADIE: He was under the car. Perhaps when I pulled him out—

CHIEF: Did he have it up on jacks? It coulda fell on him.

HECK: Naw, you don't need to jack this one up—he used to crawl under it all the time.

CHIEF: We takes our pleasure where we finds it.

SADIE: What's that supposed to mean?

CHIEF: Nothing. A little joke.

SADIE: We don't pay you to joke.

CHIEF: Mrs. Munro, with all great respect, you don't pay me nothing to do nothing. *(Noticing something about her foot.)* Now whyncha come over here and tell me where he was when you found him?

SADIE *hesitates, then comes around.* CHIEF *sees earring, as does* NEIL.

And while you're at it, disconfuse me about the times.

HECK: He was alive at 7:00. I came out and he was doing repairs, so I told him I was walking to work.

CHIEF: And you found him when?

SADIE: Around 8:30.

CHIEF: And he was under the car.

SADIE: But for his feet. I called for him and he didn't answer. When I realized he was dead, I pulled him out. It was easy enough. He was lying on the tarp and I just pulled on it—

CHIEF: *(Points at the earring that SADIE had been standing on.)* Pick that up, lad. I don't lean down too good after breakfast. Even half a breakfast.

NEIL hands earring to CHIEF.

This yours, Ma'am?

SADIE: It must've fallen off when I pulled Lee out.

HECK: So what do you think, Chief? Heart attack?

CHIEF: Well, I dunno, Heck. This Lee fella crawls under your Packard and dies. Kinda odd in my books.

HECK: What's so odd about it?

CHIEF: It just don't seem to happen every day. If I had a lotta Chinamen crawling under cars and dying, say, at a rate of, uh, one a week, I wouldn't think it was so odd. I'd say it was a trend. If there was two a week, I'd call it an epidemic and I'd quarantine 'em in the laundry. But funny thing, I can't remember the last time a Chinaman behaved this way. Or an Irishman, for that matter. Or an Albanian or a plumber (or a teacher)

SADIE: Can we send for Wilkie now?

CHIEF: Bit early for the mortician, ma'am. Think we need a visit from the coroner first.

HECK: That's unnecessary.

CHIEF: No doubt it is. But last time I forgot to call in the coroner, his feelings were hurt so bad he got his pal the newspaper editor to write an editorial about sloppy police work.

SADIE: But to leave Lee lying there—

CHIEF: Leave him be, Mrs. Munro.

SADIE: At least let me cover him.

CHIEF: Leave him be.

HECK: Sadie, perhaps the Chief would like a cup of coffee. What're you writing?

NEIL: Notes, sir.

HECK: Well, don't. *(Confiscates notebook.)* I want you to go find the bloody coroner. We'll wait for him and then have the car towed.

NEIL: *(Moving off.)* OK—now a quick phone call to thicken the plot:

BETTY is on the phone.

BETTY: I don't care what you got going, I got a coat, I got a necklace, I got a brand new Philco that picks up Boston after midnight. And someday, I'm gonna get a husband outa this. So you stay away, you and your scams. S'all I need is Heck looking out the window and see you oiling up my stairs. Don't wreck this for me. *(Hangs up.)*

NEIL: And then Christine bursts into the Y Coffee Shop.

CHRISTINE: Now?

NEIL: Yes.

CHRISTINE: I thought school would never end!

NEIL: Honey, you won't believe (what happened)

CHRISTINE: Oh Neil, I've been dying to tell you (all day long)

NEIL: First, let (me tell you)

CHRISTINE: No, me first! Please! It's so—bizarre!

NEIL: I don't know if I can cope with any more bizarre today.

CHRISTINE: Neil!

NEIL: OK, shoot.

CHRISTINE: Last night, after I'd finished cleaning Bloom's, I was taking all the supplies to the basement, to the storage room.

NEIL: I told you not to go down there by yourself.

CHRISTINE: It's not so scary.

NEIL: You said the lights weren't working.

CHRISTINE: You'll be glad I did when I tell you what happened. I was sure I heard water and I thought, "Oh flap, what if a pipe's burst!" So I shone the flashlight at the back.

Two flashlights appear on another part of the stage, more or less mirroring her description.

NEIL: So was there a flood?

CHRISTINE: Dry as the Sahara! But have you ever had something catch your eye and you never know in a million years why it does? Like—remember at the Ex when we were stuck at the top of the ferris wheel and I looked down and, out of hundreds of people, I saw Uncle Jerry going into the stripper tent? I saw a loose brick in the foundation!

NEIL: A loose brick.

CHRISTINE: Isn't that the limit! It's pitch dark and I see a loose brick!

NEIL: Is that it? I mean, a loose brick isn't exactly earth-shattering.

CHRISTINE: I pulled it out, shone my light in—

TERRY: *(Unseen.)* There's nothing here!

CHRISTINE: And there was a box there, a metal box, a cash box!

TERRY: *(Unseen.)* I'll kill that Jew!

CHRISTINE: It was locked and I couldn't get the dratted thing open so I took it home and this morning I swiped Mom's nail file and prised it apart and GUESS WHAT WAS IN IT! *(Remembers she's in public.)* Guess guess guess guess—

NEIL: Uh, papers, sales receipts—

CHRISTINE: Forty-two thousand dollars!

NEIL: What!

CHRISTINE: FORTY-TWO THOUSAND dollars! In cash. Small bills, big bills, forty-two thousand!

NEIL: (But Christine!)

CHRISTINE: Isn't it wonderful! It's like a blessing on our marriage!

NEIL: It would be if it was our money.

CHRISTINE: I found it!

NEIL: On Bloom's property. It's Mr. Bloom's.

CHRISTINE: Uh uh. This is abandoned money, lost money, money with no owner! It's not Mr. Bloom's—he's never lost a penny. He keeps everything in his office safe.

NEIL: It sounds more like "hidden money." Christine—you have to take it back. It's not yours. If it makes you feel better, we can ask a lawyer but, in the meantime, you *must* put it back.

CHRISTINE: You know what your problem is? You're pigheaded!

NEIL: I'm not pigheaded, I'm honest!

CHRISTINE: In your case it's the same thing!

The bulldozers—loud. SADIE appears with picket sign.

SADIE: STOP! STOP! THIS IS INDECENT! STOP!

The bulldozers go silent.

CHRISTINE: They stopped!

LAND: You did it!

SADIE: It's just their coffee break. They'll be back. *(Moves off.)*

WILKIE: But we've still got time.

HECK: If The Kid hurries.

NEIL: *(To Audience.)* OK, I'll jump ahead a bit—to tonight. Betty Warner's rooms on Water.

HECK: We can jump further ahead than that.

BETTY: Don't you dare! *(To Audience.)* I want you to see my "type" having her big moment of happiness.

BETTY is hugging HECK and feeling his blazer pocket. HECK is laughing.

There's something in here…

HECK: Aw, how'd you know?

BETTY: I got a sixth sense for presents. Jewellery?

HECK: No.

BETTY: A silk scarf? *(Pulls packet out.)* What is it—tickets?

HECK: Tickets. You and me. To see *South Pacific.*

BETTY: But that's in New York.

HECK: Uh huh.

BETTY: Oh, Heck. *(Quite overwhelmed; any toughness vanishes.)* That's real nice. That's real—nice. New York. A show. And a hotel? We're staying at a hotel?

HECK: The Pierre.

BETTY: *(Recovering.)* And all I gotta do is sleep with you?

HECK: Anything more would be illegal.

BETTY: *(Kissing him.)* Anything less would be unethical.

Dinner at the Copelands'.

JEAN: Are you home this evening?

ARCHIE: Yes.

JEAN: No fun and games at Bloom's?

ARCHIE: I'm never going back.

JEAN: I've heard that before.

ARCHIE: I swear.

JEAN: And we all know what your slimy word is worth. We're broke, flat broke. Listen. I've talked to a real estate agent about the front lawn and if we sever it for a gas station we can get enough to keep the house.

ARCHIE: Wait—the front lawn?

JEAN: All the frontage along Water Street. It's prime land for a service station. Everyone driving north will stop for gas.

ARCHIE: A gas station?

JEAN: We can keep the house and the land along the river. I need your signature... *(Pause.)* And then I want a divorce.

ARCHIE: No.

JEAN: It's the only way I can legally protect what little I have left. *(To Audience.)* Can you believe the laws then!

ARCHIE: You're making me a desperate man.

JEAN: What have you made me! You're a spineless disgrace! I hate you, Archie. Oh GOD, how I hate you. I could kill you, but hopefully, you'll do it to yourself. If you want more ham, you can get your own. It's on the counter. And you haven't taken your cod liver oil pill yet. One at breakfast—is that (so bloody hard to remember)

ARCHIE has exited. JEAN puts face in hands, then looks up and addresses Audience.

For the record, I could never kill him. No sooner would I get my hands around his chicken-neck and be squeezing the life out of him than I'd remember the Archie I married. He was kind of grand, that Archie. It wasn't so long ago, either—but long enough for him to become—that. And not enough time for me to forget. *(To Neil.)* If you had an ounce of decency, Mr. Novelist, you'd start back then. So they'd understand.

At the funeral home. WILKIE now has a touch of mascara.

SADIE: I've come to sit with Lee.

WILKIE: He's at Asher and Tunney.

SADIE: What?

WILKIE: They're doing him.

SADIE: But I sent him here.

WILKIE shrugs.

You've always done my family.

WILKIE: He's not quite family, is he?

SADIE: What's that supposed to mean?

WILKIE: I don't do Chinamen.

Pause.

SADIE: You are doing Lee.

WILKIE: You can't order me. If I don't want to do Chinks, I won't do them. I don't do Chinks, I don't do Darkies, I don't do Jews, I don't (do Catholics)

SADIE: Who the hell's left?

WILKIE: People like you.

SADIE: *(Indicates impatience with this to Audience, then tries Tactic One.)* I had Lee brought here because you're the best.

WILKIE: We agree on something.

SADIE: And you've always done my family. My mother—

WILKIE: Your mother…

SADIE: I remember so clearly what you did with her despite the terrible way she'd lived her life.

WILKIE: Lucky I don't have to embalm internal organs.

SADIE: Pardon?

WILKIE: Your mother's liver must've looked like Swiss cheese.

SADIE: (Yes, yes)

WILKIE: Heck could probably have driven his Packard through it.

SADIE: (Oh well)

WILKIE: Hell, they could've flown the Enola Gay through your ma's liver. "What was that we just passed through, captain?" "Sir, that was a liver."

SADIE: *(Tactic Two.)* What're you afraid of?

WILKIE: I'm not afraid of anything.

SADIE: Oh, you've got a fine reputation among those of us with white skin and light hair, but we're all pretty much the same on a slab. Lee, on the other hand—he'd be a challenge.

WILKIE: Nothing I (couldn't handle)

SADIE: I wonder what skin tones you'd use for someone like him?

WILKIE: It's no mystery.

SADIE: And his straight black hair. With Irish hair, like mine, it's all over the place, it leaves you a margin of error. But Lee's would have to be perfect—he combed it so meticulously. Hair by hair, it seemed. And then—and then, there's the matter of his concussion.

WILKIE: *(Very interested.)* There was trauma?

SADIE: Oh yes, a nasty dint on his forehead.

WILKIE: *(Tsks.)*

SADIE: God knows how they'll fix that at Asher and Tunney.

WILKIE: They'll paste his hair over it, likely. That's what they did to that lad who got hit by the train. They just pulled his hair down over his forehead and glued it. Like this. He looked like Baby Hitler.

SADIE: But you—you could cover Lee's bruises with grace and comb his hair and dress him so that all the people who come to see him will say—once again—"Wilkie is an artist."

WILKIE: I don't do Chinamen.

SADIE: *(Tactic Three.)* If you don't do Lee, I'll make damn sure your doorway is never darkened by another person—like me, like anyone else. Because this community will think twice about entrusting their loved ones to your kind—your ilk—if they ever find out where you go at night, who you go with, what it is you do with them.

WILKIE: I won't be (pushed around.)

SADIE: I'm suggesting that the next time you're caught in the park or at the bus station with your pants down, Heck may just print your name in *The Gazette.* You send your car over to Asher and Tunney; you bring Lee here. Now.

Evening. NEIL is walking CHRISTINE home.

NEIL: If Christine's said it once, she's said it a hundred times: she loves me for being decent and honest—but watch this: *(To CHRISTINE.)* You mad at me?

CHRISTINE: Why would I be mad at you?

NEIL: You haven't spoken in six blocks.

CHRISTINE: I detest idle chatter.

NEIL: You're sulking.

CHRISTINE: I hate it when I know you know you think you know you're right, and I know I'm not sure I think I know if you're right or if actually I know your thinking is wrong.

NEIL: *(After he's figured that out.)* At least put the money back until we talk to a lawyer. If it is forgotten treasure, it'll be there next week and you can have the fun of finding it all over again.

CHRISTINE: Don't patronize me. Listen, you don't have to walk me the rest of the way; go in there and finish your silly article on crime waves—

NEIL: You are mad.

CHRISTINE: I just think it's odd that you care more about old ladies lying on the pavement without their purses than your own fiancée who just found forty-two thousand dollars behind a wall. Money which would buy a cottage and a new car and a house with no basement—

NEIL: We'd feel guilty for the rest of our lives!

CHRISTINE: I wouldn't!

NEIL: Of course you would!

CHRISTINE: Would not!

NEIL: Would too!

CHRISTINE: So what if we feel guilty! I'll carry that burden for the both of us. Oh please Neil, let's just take the money.

NEIL: I'll make it up to you, I promise. Give me a kiss?

CHRISTINE: *(Gives him a peck.)* You want anything better, it's going to cost you forty-two thousand. Hey, you never told me why your day was so bad.

NEIL: Oh God—you'll never believe it—Heck Munro's driver was found dead in their garage.

CHRISTINE: Lee?

NEIL: How d'you know him?

CHRISTINE: He's Mr. Bloom's best friend—they're like brothers! How?

NEIL: The coroner took one look and said heart failure. But Lee had a concussion, too. The coroner's theory is he had a heart attack when he was under the car fixing it. He reared up suddenly, hit his head—

CHRISTINE: Oh, I feel terrible! Here I've been gloating over our windfall and all this time poor Lee's... Why didn't you interrupt me when I was blathering about the money? You go on up and finish your story and I'll walk home. I'll see you tomorrow.

Light on TERRY. He's leaning against BETTY's door—street level—finishing a cigarette.

NEIL: Naw. I'm gonna walk you home.

Black. Clock alarms. Light comes up on NEIL, who is in the newsroom, working.

Day Two, 7:30 A.M.—and The Kid is hard at work. *(Sotto.)* On my novel. "Dorothy's eyes rolled upwards and she contemplated God as a grey rain plocked down." That's my opening line. Christine doesn't like it.

CHRISTINE: *(To Audience.)* It reeks of Hemingway.

NEIL: *(To Audience.)* So.

HECK enters.

HECK: Morning, Kid. Updating that series on the purse snatchings? Look I want you to go over to the garage and see if the car's ready. If it is, bring it back. There's no trick to driving a Packard—just leave lots of room on either side.

HECK exits. NEIL turns; he is at the garage, with the CHIEF. They are both looking up.

NEIL: What're you looking for?

CHIEF: I thought I'd take a gander at the underside of what my betters drive. Wondrous creations, cars, especially Packards. This must be how God sees us.

NEIL: He'd be looking down, sir.

CHIEF: Depends what time of the year. Earth rotates. Half the year God's looking down on Australia—which means He's looking up right up our arses.

NEIL: Sir, why do you think Lee was under the car?

CHIEF: I honestly don't know.

NEIL: Repairs?

CHIEF: Doubt it.

NEIL: But Mrs. Munro said—

CHIEF: I know what she said. Oh, there could be any number of reasons, of the mechanical sort. If there are, the boys here will find 'em. There's a story behind this car. Heck won it from Archie Copeland. Ever hear that?

NEIL: No, but Mr. Munro (would never tell me)

CHIEF: Poker. Archie bet the Packard with two pair, jacks high. The car was his wife's. You know, I can't for the life of me see anyplace on the underside of this chassis where that poor lad having a heart attack might've reared up and hit his head. If that moron of a coroner was right and it was a heart attack. And I dunno why Sadie Munro spent all that time standing with her foot over her earring. Kinda disrespectful of jewellery.

NEIL: Mrs. Munro told you she found him at 8:30 but she didn't call us at the paper until 9:00.

CHIEF: That so? You know, Kid, I can be real grateful for details like that.

NEIL demurs, under.

"Scoop Griffin"—has a nice ring. That cheap bastard you work for'll be obliged to give you a raise.

NEIL: He's actually quite generous—

CHIEF: I don't like Heck Munro. Don't like his editorials, his politics, don't like none of them stuck-up pricks living up Water. Never did, never will. OK, I guess that's enough gawking at Packards for one morning. It ain't ready yet—can I give you a lift downtown? You can tell me about that fiancée of yours.

NEIL: How'd you even know I had one?

CHIEF: Christine's minister told me. I hear she's going to be a teacher. That's a fine occupation. Twist all them little young minds. *(Exiting.)* Teachers and preachers. Twist, twist, twist.

The Minister's study at First Presbyterian.

SADIE: Reverend, if you were betrayed and, in your anger, you behaved rashly, and did something terrible—could you be forgiven?

LAND: Yes, I believe so.

SADIE: Then I'm ready.

LAND: Ready to do what?

SADIE: To confess.

LAND: Whoah! Sadie!

SADIE: What!

LAND: We're Presbyterians. We don't have confession! Not between a minister and a church member! That's something you have to do in private, thank the Lord. I couldn't cope with all those secrets. Catholic priests—the things they must hear. Who on earth do they tell?

SADIE: No one!

LAND: Everyone tells someone!

SADIE: Then they tell God.

LAND: Piffle! They whip back to the rectory and swap stories over dinner. But I doubt there's a priest alive who's more indiscreet than I am. I know you're in a terrible state with Lee's death. It's so ironic (that he died just as)

SADIE: That's another thing: Wilkie is doing the arrangements.

LAND: Wilkie means well, but I wish he wouldn't go quite so overboard. He slapped so much powder on Avery Tedford I could've sworn I was burying Marie Antoinette.

SADIE: I had to, uh, bully Wilkie. He wouldn't do Lee because he's Chinese.

LAND: I can't fathom that kind of narrow-mindedness. But what do you want me to do?

SADIE: The service, of course.

LAND: Sadie, you know I'd be happy to, but do you think Lee was Presbyterian?

SADIE: He was Buddhist.

LAND: Then shouldn't we be finding a Buddhist to bury him?

SADIE: It's all the same!

LAND: *(Mock horror.)* Don't tell my congregation!

SADIE: You're not finking out on me, are you?

LAND: *(Sigh.)* I'd never "fink" out on you, Sadie. There's no one in this church with anything like your spirituality. It's refreshing. And your stewardship of the Necropolis—

SADIE: I talk to the dead.

LAND: Yes, well, we don't exactly do that in our church either. I've read a lot about the Buddhists; they have customs, interesting ones, I've always been a bit jealous of 'em. We don't need to advertise I'm doing this but yes, I can do something. Quasi-Buddhist. But Sadie, I don't have the power to change cemetery policy.

SADIE: Meaning?

LAND: He'll have to be buried outside the fence. Beyond the pale, so to speak. *(Pause.)* Is there anything else?

SADIE: *(Pause.)* Yes.

LAND: Music for the service?

SADIE: Adultery.

LAND: Adultery?

SADIE: This is very difficult for me to talk about.

LAND: Sadie dear, don't trouble your heart. I went to see Heck. I had heard the rumours and I felt it necessary to verify. He is under a—certain—uh—hold. Some of my harsher colleagues might call it the hold of the devil. But I'd rather save the devil up for bigger things: Hitler. Mussolini. Baptists. Heck is only behaving like every red-blooded, worried man does when he reaches his age. Clergy excluded. Heck's little fling with Betty Warner—it will pass.

SADIE: I wasn't talking about Heck.

LAND: Oh.

SADIE: Who's Betty Warner?

LAND: Oh Lord.

BLOOM's store. JEAN bursts in.

JEAN: Where is he? Where's Archie?

BLOOM: He's not here.

JEAN: If he is, so help me God, I'll kill the (both of you.)

BLOOM: Mrs. Copeland—there are customers—

JEAN: Hang your customers!

BLOOM: Perhaps you'd like to (come to my office)

JEAN: Now, you listen to me. Next time Archie walks in that door, you kick him right back out.

BLOOM: I really don't know (what you're talking about)

JEAN: Or I'll blow the whistle on you so loud you won't know what hit you. You'll be back picking rags in Russia.

CHRISTINE enters. She has the cash box under her coat.

CHRISTINE: Hello! (Nice afternoon)

BLOOM: Christine, why are you here today?

CHRISTINE: I'm just going to go downstairs to check on my (cleaning supplies)

BLOOM: No, (go home)

JEAN: I could wring your neck!

BLOOM: Mrs. Copeland doesn't, uh, like her couch. Where are you going?

CHRISTINE: Downstairs. Are the lights fixed yet?

BLOOM: Please, just go home. GO! *(To JEAN.)* You too.

JEAN: Perhaps you are deriving some delight out of ruining my family. Perhaps this is some kind of Jewish revenge thing, though why you're going after my family I don't know—all we've ever done is buy your ridiculous furniture and before that leave rags out for your pathetic father. *(Wheeling to face Audience.)* And you: judge not lest ye be judged.

BLOOM: *(To Audience.)* No, please, be my guest—judge away.

JEAN: Bloom: have you ever read *The Merchant of Venice*?

BLOOM: (I, uh)

JEAN: Would you agree that Shylock is a fair representative of your race?

BLOOM: As much as Eva Braun is of yours.

JEAN: I'm Scottish. Try again.

CHRISTINE: Mr. Bloom is a kind and decent man! I'm going to graduate from teacher's college in a month and it never would have been possible but for his generosity! He's given me a job these past two years.

JEAN: Apparently *I* pay your salary! If there's anybody's generosity you should be praising, it's mine!

JEAN exits.

CHRISTINE: She should wash her mouth out with soap!

BLOOM: I'm going to close the store now.

CHRISTINE: What does she mean, she "pays my salary"?

BLOOM: I'd like you to go home.

CHRISTINE: But I want (to go downstairs)

BLOOM: NOW! Now. I'll see you tomorrow night. GO!

CHRISTINE exits.

(To Audience.) I'm not a rich man. In fact, I'm up to my ears in debt. But I give a hundred dollars to the Red

Cross. I give fifty dollars to the YMCA. I give seventy-five annually to the high school for a bursary in my mother's memory. And still that happens. *(Exiting.)* I donated five mattresses to the hospital last year. I planted ten trees along the river. No one bought more war bonds than I did!

BLOOM exits.

JEAN: I always regretted saying those things.

CHRISTINE: I regretted hearing them.

JEAN: I never went back in his store. Not from '49 till he sold it in '85. And if I saw him downtown I'd cross the street. I was that embarrassed. I had to sit beside him at the Community Concert one night and I nearly died.

CHRISTINE: Perhaps if you'd apologized—

JEAN: How can you ever apologize for saying what I said? There's no words large enough. Anyway, apologies are too easy. Everyone's apologizing for everything these days. It doesn't mean a thing. A lifetime being ashamed, that's better.

At the mortuary.

WILKIE: *(Pulls down the sheet.)* What do you think?

SADIE nods; overcome.

His skin was like marble. You were right about his hair. Look at that part. I used a ruler to get it right. And see how I've covered the bruising. You can't tell. I *was* afraid. He's different and I was afraid of that, afraid I'd fail. But I haven't. I've succeeded. He was a beautiful man; it was an honour to do him.

WILKIE can see that SADIE is crying.

I'm going to see about a few things. I'll leave you here.

WILKIE exits. SADIE leans forward and cradles LEE, pulling him up. She apologizes to him. As she does, his body becomes ever so slightly alive, then gradually loses life again as she lets him back down.

SADIE: *(During this.)* I'm sorry. I'm sorry. I'm sorry.

SADIE eventually looks up. HECK has been watching.

HECK: That's enough, Sadie. That's enough of that. Time to come home. That's enough of that, dear. Come (home, Sadie, come, dear, please)

Black. Alarms. YMCA Coffee Shop ambience. NEIL and CHIEF are having breakfast.

NEIL: Day Three and some things are starting to make sense.

CHIEF: ...OK, Scoop. Out with it. What's on your mind?

NEIL: What exactly goes on at Bloom's store?

CHIEF: Near as I can tell—the attempted sale of furniture.

NEIL: Has anyone reported money missing?

CHIEF: No. We've had a spate of purse snatchings in the north end, but you're covering that already. *(Reads.)* "Her arm was snapped from its socket like a Christmas wishbone."?

NEIL: Were you aware that Lee knew Bloom (and they)

CHIEF: You're asking me if Lee gambled. Of course he did.

NEIL: And that's OK?

CHIEF: No, but what else could he do to pass the time? You ever wonder why there's only men working in that laundry and at the Sunrise Café and all them other Chinese places? It's because we never let them poor devils bring their women here. From—when was it, early twenties—until two years ago. Something called

The Excluding Act. Excluding 'em from the connubial you-know. You get to frolic around Bloom's with your teacher—but what do they do all night? They could do Bible study, sure, maybe play some Parcheesi—but gambling's a lot more fun. There's a game every night upstairs of the Sunrise. It don't concern me.

NEIL: I mean, at Bloom's.

CHIEF: Don't forget—Lee's been here since he was a lad. His old man worked at that laundry on Aylmer and brung him over when he was six or seven. Then his dad died, so Lee's uncle, No-Tickee-No-Laundry, took over. Lee palled around with Bloom when they were kids. He wasn't like the rest of the Chinamen. He was more like us than them. So maybe he branched out. So long as nobody gets hurt—

NEIL: But someone killed Lee! You think it's murder too!

CHIEF: I'm trying hard not to think anything too definite yet. *(Looks at watch.)* 10:30. We better hightail it to the Necropolis.

NEIL: *(To Audience.)* There was only a handful of us at Lee's funeral, some from the laundry and the Sunrise Café, Max Bloom, the Munros. The interment was on the other side of the fence, unconsecrated ground reserved for indigents, suicides and non-Christians.

BLOOM: "Oh! Call my brother back to me!
I cannot play alone;
The summer comes with flower and bee—
Where is my brother gone?"

Where is my brother gone?

Mourners exit. The newsroom.

HECK: You were at the burial. Why?

NEIL: (I, uh, felt)

HECK: I asked you to interview Lee when he was alive. He's dead now; there's no story.

NEIL: (I know but)

HECK: So it's noon and you're just starting work. And I don't know what you did for work yesterday, either. That thing you filed on the purse-snatching, that was an abomination.

NEIL: But sir—you ran it.

HECK: I had space to fill. But this: "Mrs. Gillespie writhed on the ground in post-snatch agony"? And how did you know she looked up at the sky and "contemplated a God who had forsaken her"? And what the living hell is a "grey rain plocking a weary tattoo on the sidewalk"? What is this word "plocking"? What rain? This is the driest June in twenty years!

NEIL: I thought it was a strong image.

HECK: Mrs. Gillespie just phoned. She thinks you're calling her an atheist. She wants to sue. Kid: if I want flowery stuff I'll hire a goddamn novelist. Lee's funeral was private. You had no business being there.

NEIL: Sir! I have reason to believe Lee was murdered! I also believe he was operating some kind of gambling den at Bloom's store!

HECK: Your point?

NEIL: Christine found a box in Bloom's basement. Hidden behind some bricks. There was forty-two thousand dollars in it.

HECK: What!

NEIL: In bills of all denominations.

HECK: How much?

NEIL: Forty-two grand!

HECK: No slang, Kid. What'd she do with it?

NEIL: She took it. Finders keepers.

HECK: Finders keepers is for when you find a quarter on the sidewalk.

NEIL: That's how I felt. I told her we could go see a lawyer, but first she should put it back.

HECK: Has she?

NEIL: She tried yesterday, but Bloom sent her home before she had a chance. I'm going with her tonight to return it. Sir—doesn't all this seem odd to you?

HECK: I don't pay you to play detective. But I do pay you. And right now I want a follow-up on the purse thing, which includes Mrs. Gillespie's full embrace of Jesus, Mary, Joseph and the twelve disciples. Get lost.

HECK turns to talk to someone on the phone.

Forty-two thousand! Be a nice story if it wasn't such a can of worms. I told The Kid to put it back. Imagine his girlfriend finding that kind of money in someone's basement and thinking she can just waltz home with it. Now give your sugar poppa a big phone kiss.

BETTY: *(Turning to tell someone.)* The silly git finds the money; turns out Bloom's been hiding it behind a rock or something in his basement! So what does she do? She walks outa there at midnight—and takes it home!

TERRY appears on other phone.

TERRY: So that's where it is! How much did you say? Forty-two thousand! Where does she live? Oh—her boyfriend's returning it to the store—tonight?

TERRY turns to someone in shadow.

I've located the money. But my share's two-thirds now.

WILKIE's mortuary.

WILKIE: *(To Audience.)* They said I couldn't do a Chinaman, but I did. And still they snicker. I see their parents out, I see their children out, someday I'll see them out—and they snicker. This city'd happily nail me to a cross until that moment when they need me, and then they come here snivelling, begging for me to work my magic, once again. And I will. I'll work magic on all of them. But who will work his magic on me?

WILKIE reaches up and snaps light off. BLOOM's basement.

CHRISTINE: We have to be quick! Flap, the light's still out!

NEIL turns his flashlight on. CHRISTINE has the box.

BLOOM: *(From above.)* Christine! Is that you!

CHRISTINE: Oh no—that's Bloom! *(Calls.)* Yes sir! *(To NEIL.)* It's at the back.

CHRISTINE runs up the stairs, opens door; BLOOM is there.

I was just getting (some supplies)

CHRISTINE closes door. NEIL immediately snaps his flashlight on and starts moving with the box to the wall. A flashlight flickers behind him.

NEIL: Who's there! Who's there!

No answer, but maybe a sound. NEIL proceeds. The other flashlight flickers behind NEIL, who has started to replace the money. Suddenly there is a struggle. NEIL refuses to give up the cash box and is stabbed in the gut. He falls, his flashlight clattering to the floor.

Christine! Christine!

CHRISTINE and BLOOM open the door to basement, and light floods in. TERRY is at the top of the stairs.

TERRY: Outa my way!

BLOOM: (What the hell!)

TERRY pushes by BLOOM, struggling with him. CHRISTINE runs down to NEIL, who is dying.

CHRISTINE: NEIL!

The cash box is by NEIL's side. CHRISTINE is screaming; upstairs BLOOM has chased TERRY off.

NEIL: *(To Audience.)* If I'd been a poet I might have gasped out something short and fine to Christine. And if I'd been a real novelist instead of a poser, well, I could have left Christine with an entire paragraph of love. But I'm just a reporter, a cheesy guy who, when confronted by the final act of his life—with all the dramatic and poetic implications that offers—turns pragmatic. *(To CHRISTINE.)* Take the money!

Fast Black.

End of Act One

Act Two

Stage is black. Dawn sears across the back. The alarms start again—this time, modern: beepers and coffee makers and car alarms and watches and burbling cellphones—perhaps even muffled traffic reports. The citizens walk to their chairs in the rising light.

ALL: *(Audible now, not in unison, repeated as they move to seats.)* We are the dead... (etc.)

Growing up and under this, the sound of bulldozers. For the first time, the sound should be clearly identifiable as such. When everyone—with the exception of SADIE*—has taken their seats, the sounds cut out. Lights up. As* NEIL *talks, there is response and rhubarb from the dead, under.*

NEIL: Welcome back! In case you didn't read your programme, the setting has changed slightly—from Water Street generally, to—specifically—the Ashburnham Necropolis. From a city of many thousands of humans, living, breathing, dreaming, embalming, gambling, selling mattresses, making love on mattresses—

CHRISTINE: Neil!

NEIL: What?

CHRISTINE: Excuse me, my reputation?

NEIL: We're dead. Who cares what they think? *(Back to Audience.)* At intermission, some of you talked about your kids and your jobs and one gentleman—blue sweater, pony tail…

CHIEF: Pony tail?

NEIL: You told your mistress you were leaving her for your wife.

BETTY: Yeah, we know that ugly tune. Where is the bastard? Point him (out and I'll—)

HECK holds her back.

NEIL: And another gentleman—I'll be more discreet which—you told your wife you were leaving her—for a man!

JEAN: I only wish I'd been that lucky.

NEIL: Eighteen of you snuck outside, to smoke. Why outside?

BETTY: And listen, I bummed one at intermission. I don't know what's with cigs nowadays—you gotta suck on 'em like you're a vacuum.

CHRISTINE: Lucky you had all that training.

BETTY: Look who's talking.

The dead enjoy this, but are getting restless again.

NEIL: Some of you speculated about who killed the Chinaman. Actually, only one of you said "Chinaman" and that was to comment disparagingly on me saying it in the first act. The rest of you all politely said "Lee" or "Mr. Kwan."

One or two of the dead have begun motioning for LEE to join them. They will increase their efforts. BLOOM eventually tries to physically pull him in.

Generally, the women favour Mr. Munro as the culprit.

HECK: That's absurd.

NEIL: But the men are blaming—in descending order—Betty, Sadie, Jean and Christine.

BETTY, JEAN and CHRISTINE all react with indignation as their names are spoken.

CHRISTINE: Anything in a skirt.

NEIL: And you, the man in the pony tail, you bet your now-former mistress a fin that no one did it. You said this'd be another one of those evenings at the theatre that peters out into significant nothingness.

JEAN: It'll get bulldozed into nothingness if you don't shake a leg.

HECK: Give them a quick description first of the Necropolis, so they won't think it's just a bunch of chairs.

NEIL: They understand that.

HECK: It's Sadie's life's work. Tell them, Kid.

NEIL: Yes, sir.

JEAN: Quickly.

NEIL: The Necropolis—in addition to being a cemetery—is an arboretum. For years, Sadie Munro chaired a committee, they planted all sorts of trees that shouldn't grow this far north.

LAND: Dear poor Sadie wanted to create a Carolinian forest at the very edge of the Shield. And look. *(Indicates.)* A northern Eden.

BETTY: We make good fertilizer.

NEIL: That's a mulberry—very popular with the raccoons—magnolia, chestnut. The one shedding bark is a London Plane.

WILKIE: We call it our "dirty tree."

JEAN: Imagine, a bunch of corpses calling a tree dirty.

BLOOM: Don't you think he should've done all this descriptive stuff in the first act? When he was talking about the city—

BETTY: Can you imagine what his novel would've been like? All back to front.

ARCHIE: All the action in the first chapter, then nothing but adjectives for a thousand pages.

WILKIE: That's like embalming someone before they die!

LAND: Or like dying before you've been saved!

BETTY: Or being saved before you've had a chance to live!

NEIL: OK, OK. *(Back to Audience, and over mounting rhubarb and exertions by others to get* LEE *into play.)* You've probably noticed we have a bit of an imperative here. Our lives—our past-lives—our post-lives—are about to change. But we have an unsolved murder. I have an uncompleted novel. This is currently a play without an ending. Without that, we're a city without closure.

JEAN: "Closure"?

NEIL: That is, unless I can masterfully pull together the disparate strands in this web of desire and deceit. Thus bringing us to a conclusion as to who killed Lee Kwan. Thus illuminating the universe. Thus solving conclusively what exactly God sees when he looks down on the Australians and up our arses!

LEE bounds on.

LEE: *Thus* enters the Chinaman!

Applause and cheers from all, except NEIL and HECK. Rhubarb from all, including:

BETTY: About time, you dope.

JEAN: Neil's been droning on.

LAND: Praise the Lord!

CHRISTINE: It really is Lee!

Rhubarb ends.

WILKIE: How do you like him?

CHRISTINE: You did a nice job. What'd you use?

WILKIE: A peach base with mahogany highlights.

NEIL: OK, OK.

CHIEF: *(To LEE.)* Son, I need to ask you a few questions—

NEIL: Hey—

LEE: Sure, Chief, fire away. Fire away, get it?

JEAN: Oh great, he's a comedian.

NEIL: HEY! HEY!

LEE: Hey, what?

NEIL: What are you doing here?

LEE: It's my story.

JEAN: Excuse us?

NEIL: It's *our* story. But I'm telling it.

LEE: Oh, that's fair. I'm the one who gets murdered. I spend the entire First Act lying under a Packard with my frigging feet sticking out, but you get to tell the story.

NEIL: I'm sorry, Lee. I know it's your life, your murder (but that doesn't)

HECK: Murder hasn't been established.

NEIL: But it doesn't automatically make you the best one to tell it.

LEE: I knew you'd say that.

NEIL: Well, there's a certain arc to these things, which I, as a would-be novelist, understand and you, as a chauffeur, don't. To put this in chauffeur terms, you can't drive to the truth of something without going on a bit of a road trip.

HECK: Patronizing bugger.

NEIL: Especially when we're talking murder. You have to collect things: a motive, opportunity, a prime suspect. You just can't say, "Lee was killed by…"

CHIEF: Why not?

Pause.

NEIL: What?

CHIEF: Just ask him.

LEE: Yeah, just ask me who killed me, Mr. Would-be Novelist.

BETTY: I want to know if it's Terry.

TERRY: It wasn't me! 'Course my "type" is prone to lying.

WILKIE: Ask him, so we can go. Speaking professionally, I would prefer you all get to your new resting place—well rested.

CHIEF: I'm not going anywhere—I can't go anywhere—until I know. It's my one unsolved case—

HECK: It's not a "case."

BLOOM: I've never stopped feeling guilty.

LAND: I truly fear it was Sadie.

HECK: Stuff a sock in it!

CHIEF: Please—we need to know!

The others murmur in agreement. NEIL looks at LEE and shrugs.

NEIL: OK, OK. So much for the art of storytelling. *(To the Audience.)* Gather up your purses and your coats and get ready to meander home after just what—five minutes—of a rather squalid Second Act. Because we're about to reveal the juicy nub of this play in one quick, efficient headline: Lee—Kwan—was—killed—by…

LEE: I don't know.

JEAN: What do you mean "You don't know"!

LEE: I don't know.

CHRISTINE: We know who killed Neil.

LEE: I can't remember.

NEIL: I remember that punk over there shanking me in the gut.

TERRY: "Shanked"? What're you reading?

LEE: I don't know who killed me. It must've been from behind.

TERRY: I don't "shank" from behind.

LEE: Then I've got amnesia.

TERRY: I don't give amnesia to nobody.

LEE: Anyway, I didn't get stabbed. *(Pulls up shirt.)* Look, no marks.

TERRY: I always leave marks.

WILKIE: You did have that nasty concussion I covered so well.

HECK: That was from my Packard.

CHIEF: I doubt that was enough to kill him.

LEE: I honestly don't remember anything.

NEIL: Do any of you know?

There's silence. BETTY gives TERRY the eye, and he looks away.

Fine. So now do you think you can all just shut up and let me tell this my way?

WILKIE: Be our guest—

BETTY: It's your big break—

CHRISTINE: Mr. Hemingway.

Sound of bulldozers. SADIE enters with a picket sign.

BETTY: Aw hell, why's she here! She's not even one of us yet!

SADIE: Do I make you nervous, "Zig"?

BETTY: I just don't think it's fair you're always hanging about before your time. You're a dead woman wannabe. And how is it you can talk to us?

LAND: She has the power. I'm happy for her, but it gives me the theological willies.

SADIE: I'm trying to save you. All of you.

BETTY: We know why you're here—you (want a little nookie with)

HECK: Betty—that's enough!

BETTY: Anyway, we don't need saving.

NEIL: Actually, we do. Physically. *(To Audience.)* It's kind of involved. The city to the south—it's been growing north.

LAND: *(To Audience.)* Most nights all we can see in the sky now is an orange glow. I worry that when the Messiah comes again, we'll never see the star.

JEAN: *(To Audience.)* They made Water Street one way—south this time, Betty—then they widened it.

WILKIE: They even had to move your statue.

BLOOM: They were dying for an excuse to get rid of it.

NEIL: *(To Audience.)* The final act of Ashburnham's planner was to take a ruler and draw a sensible six-lane line, right through here. So everyone can go there, from there—through us.

LAND: *(To Audience.)* We're in the way. Oh, there were protests.

JEAN: *(To Audience.)* But local democracy doesn't carry any weight anymore.

SADIE: *(To Audience.)* We've been amalgamated into silence.

NEIL: *(To Audience.)* We have to leave. *(To SADIE.)* How are we fixed for time ma'am?

SADIE: We've still got a bit. A TV crew from the metropolis has shown up and they want a shot of me with the bulldozers. They're hoping I'll lie under one. I can stall them. If you start now—and if the rest of you don't interrupt—you can finish in time.

NEIL: OK. 1949. My funeral. Positions. Lee, you have to watch from the unconsecrated area, sorry. Mr. Munro, you first. Mrs. Munro, you'll have to stay for this part—

Mourners begin lining up behind HECK. WILKIE escorts NEIL, fussing over the body. BETTY and TERRY are not present. LEE watches from a distance.

CHIEF: Sharp as a tack he was.

WILKIE: A wonderful specimen but for the gashed gut.

LAND: A fine Christian lad.

BLOOM: Why he and Christine were down in my basement beats me.

CHIEF: Two murders in three days.

HECK: One murder.

CHRISTINE: Forty-two thousand. I'd swap it all for just one more hour with him. *(But then, in wonderment.)* Forty-two thousand!

SADIE: What on earth did you do to his eyes!

WILKIE: Are you second-guessing me?

SADIE: No, but at the funeral home I looked and—you've made him—almost—

WILKIE: I'm in my Chinese period now.

CHRISTINE: Shh—Mr. Munro's going to speak.

HECK: *(Eulogizing.)* He reminded me of me. He was hungry for the story, a born reporter. Questioned everything he saw. Except, of course, the existence of God. I have no doubt that as he lay on the floor of Bloom's basement, gushing blood, the tears of Jesus plocked gently down on Water.

NEIL: Hey.

HECK: Knowing The Kid, he probably took notes. Added a lot of adjectives.

NEIL: Hey!

HECK: Called it a story. Brought it in under deadline.

NEIL: Hey!

LEE: He can't hear you.

NEIL: He's making fun of me! At my own funeral!

LEE: At least you got a half-decent turnout. There's over a hundred here. And Mr. Munro's not really making fun of you. He knew about your novel; he was kinda proud. He used to joke about it on the way to work. "There's a purple haze over the newsroom—The Kid's at it again."

The sound of bulldozers starting up. The mourners all turn to NEIL *expectantly.* SADIE *hurries off in the direction of the sound.*

SADIE: *(Exiting.)* Stop! Stop that! Save our dead!

A few of them make "get going" motions with their hands.

NEIL: What?

CHIEF: Keep it moving! *(To Audience.)* This is my favourite part.

NEIL: My assassin didn't get far. He struggled with Max Bloom at the top of the stairs, pushed him aside and ran through the—plocking—rain, down Water to Betty's.

TERRY *appears, running.*

TERRY: Lemme in!

BETTY: What the hell!

TERRY: I need a clean shirt!

BETTY: What've you done now!

TERRY: Get me a shirt!

BETTY: You're bleeding!

TERRY: Doesn't that rich guy keep a shirt here?

BETTY: I'll get a bandage—

TERRY: It ain't my blood.

BETTY: Oh, great.

TERRY: What—you prefer it's mine!

BETTY: What've you done!

TERRY: Just hand me the shirt. How much money have you got?

BETTY: Not much.

TERRY: Give it to me.

BETTY: Here—twenty bucks.

TERRY: Thanks, sis. *(To Audience.)* And I woulda got away, if it hadn't been for the Night Crawler.

Everyone looks automatically at WILKIE.

WILKIE: OK, OK. It just so happened I was out on the street.

JEAN: Bit late for a stroll, Wilkie.

WILKIE: I have nerves.

JEAN: We can just imagine.

WILKIE: Walking calms them. *(To CHIEF.)* He ran in there!

CHIEF appears with gun.

CHIEF: Hold it right there, both of you. Hands up.

TERRY and BETTY raise their hands.

(To Audience.) It's not loaded. Never has been. Not even the time I nabbed him in Madoc.

TERRY: What!

CHIEF: A loaded gun'd scare the jeezly breakfast right outa me.

LAND: Everyone in town knows it's unloaded. *(To Audience.)* I even preached a sermon on it once. "A man without faith is like Chief Bromell's unloaded gun."

TERRY: Aw, damn!

LAND: See—if you'd been going to church you'd still be a free man.

CHIEF: Move on out, gang.

BETTY: *(As they leave.)* Thanks loads, Tare.

CHIEF: Get going.

CHIEF stops by the grieving CHRISTINE.

Dear, I know this is difficult for you, but I need to know why you had that money, in a box, in Bloom's basement, under your sweater.

CHRISTINE: I found it, a couple of nights ago—

BLOOM: It was in my store.

CHIEF: You're saying it was yours?

BLOOM: No, I'm only saying it was in my store. Therefore, it's mine.

CHRISTINE: It's mine! Finders keepers.

BLOOM: You found it on my property!

CHRISTINE: Possession is nine-tenths of the law. Mr. Munro—I'd like you to print this in *The Gazette*: "In memory of

Neil Griffin I'm giving half of this to Ashburnham High, for scholarships for the needy." *(To BLOOM.)* You wouldn't deny our young scholars twenty-one thousand dollars, would you?

BLOOM: You ungrateful guttersnipe! Have you forgotten who gave you a job so you could afford to go to teachers' college? *(To CHIEF.)* I'm launching a lawsuit. So what if she "found" it—it was my wall, my brick, my building, therefore it's (my money)

CHIEF: I dunno, Maxie. What about all them needy young scholars?

BLOOM: Never mind them. *(To HECK.)* I'm giving half to, uh, the orphans of war.

CHIEF: Maybe we could give her half to the students, your half to the orphans, send Terry to the slammer, put the empty box back in the wall and wait for a few years. See if it refills.

BLOOM: It's my money!

ARCHIE is hiding behind a newspaper. JEAN punches it.

JEAN: How much of it is mine!

ARCHIE doesn't answer.

That does it. I'm calling the Chief.

ARCHIE: Don't. Jean—

JEAN starts to leave.

Jean, GET BACK HERE!

JEAN—in utter amazement—stops.

We have no money, no island, no silver, no china. In one week our front lawn will be a Fina station. All we have left is your reputation. If you start meddling in this, we won't even have that.

Focus back on LEE and NEIL. They are sharing cigarettes.

NEIL: Wild guess. It was your cash?

LEE: Does it matter?

SADIE returns. She puts down her protest sign and does a little star turn.

SADIE: I'm a star! I laid my ancient carcass down in front of those shovels and the cameras couldn't get enough of me. No newspapers, by the way. Just television. A real alphabet soup of stations. Neil: the barbarians are at the gates. Your novel needs condensing, and now. *(Over NEIL's protests.)* It's 1949. It's two days after your burial and a week after Lee's. Quiet! Please. *(Holds up flowers; to Audience.)* You'll notice these are hothouse. Ashburnham Floral Supply. I can no longer get to the island to pick wild ones; I won't learn how to drive until Heck dies in 1970. *(To the others.)* Get in your places.

NEIL really protests.

Whose wife am I? Good. Now stand there. Oh God. Here goes. *(To LEE.)* How does one ever apologize for killing someone?

LEE: What!?

NEIL: *(To Audience.)* OK, this is coming a little earlier than I had planned, but you do remember my doubts back in the first act—and, and that earring on the ground and—and the general aura of guilt at the Munros'—*(Notices that SADIE is waiting for him to stop talking.)* Sorry, ma'am.

SADIE: How does one ever apologize for killing someone? But to get that phone call from Reverend Land—

LEE: What phone call!

NEIL: I kind of skipped over it.

SADIE: I never meant to—I was lashing out—if you'd come out from under there and actually faced me... Now: I can't sleep, I can't go to the police, I can't tell Heck the truth, he'd have to put it on his own front page. His own wife, a murderer. And here I am, still respecting him enough to hold all this in, to not go to the police... I'll go to my grave stinking of guilt. I'll spend my life making useless acts of contrition, sweeping your grave, planting it, cleaning your stone... Lee, you don't have to worry about your "friend." I'm packing your things. I'll send everything back to China, and if there's money, that can go too. But I'm not sending you.

SADIE leaves.

NEIL: *(To Audience.)* This is the biggest story that has ever hit this green and pleasant town! AND GODDAMMIT, I CAN'T FILE IT. I'M DEAD! She killed you!

LEE: No.

NEIL: She just said she did!

LEE: It's not possible.

CHIEF ambles over.

CHIEF: Technically, I can't say this to you until I die, in 1967—but I think you ought to hear this now. A good cop is never fooled by the obvious. If something's obvious, you haven't used your noggin. Sure, we got a confession—but we also got a victim that says:

LEE: I never saw her that morning. I'm sure of it. Never saw her, never heard her.

CHIEF: Yup, yup, yup. It's all so obvious, I can't figure the damn thing out. Why would a woman confess something she didn't do?—unless she's covering for someone. *(Looks at HECK.)* Now wouldn't that be rich? But maybe that's too obvious, too.

SADIE returns. She is now holding wildflowers.

LEE: Why're you—why's she—

NEIL: You just brought him flowers.

SADIE: These are ones I picked. I'm going back further in time.

NEIL: I don't know. Mrs. Munro—you've confessed and that pretty much wraps up my story, albeit a bit prematurely.

SADIE: You still need a motive. And to establish that, we have to go to my island. Back two years.

LEE: No!

SADIE: To 1947.

LEE: This cannot be told!

SADIE: I need them to understand. Completely. Be fair. When I die there won't be anyone left to explain. If they understand how it all started—well, they'll leave here, they'll go back to their cars and drive up Water and when they go past my house, my garage or—or past *The Gazette* or Wilkie's, or the church—Archie and Jean's—everything's going to look a little different and they'll thank you for it. I know they will. And they might even forgive me. You owe me this. Please.

LEE reluctantly nods assent.

As I said, it started in 1947, early May. If we'd known about global warming then we might have been worried because it was gloriously hot. Lee and I were up at my island, just the two of us—

LEE: And a million blackflies.

SADIE: We were picking flowers for the Necropolis.

LEE: And mosquitoes.

SADIE: And it struck me: all this time, Lee had been driving me north and south and back and forth across town and I didn't really know the first thing about him. *(To LEE.)* Is there someone—special—you'd like to take flowers back to?

LEE is mortified.

You must have a girlfriend—

LEE: No.

SADIE: Oh, come on. In all of Ashburnham there's not (one girl)

LEE: No. *(To Audience.)* A girlfriend? Is she blind? In Ashburnham? *(To NEIL.)* There were no women for us.

NEIL: You were all virgins?

LEE: *(Steering him off a bit.)* No, you idiot—we'd go the city, sometimes, once a month—we'd go to the prostitutes in Chinatown. There were some who'd take our money—

SADIE: Tell them what you said next.

LEE is objecting.

Please. "Max Bloom's mother—"

LEE: Max Bloom's mother—she's dying.

SADIE: I've heard.

LEE: I'd like to take some flowers to her. I beg you, stop this, stop here.

SADIE: *(To NEIL.)* I have an image you could've used in your novel if you'd lived. A woman. Her eyes are clamped shut. Like she's willfully blind. And then she feels gentle fingers on her lids, pushing them open. This is what he did for me. *(To LEE.)* "Max is my only friend. My only real friend." *(Repeats.)* "My only real friend."

LEE: *(Over latter; to SADIE.)* My only real friend. When I was a boy, he was the only one who asked me to his house, ever. And Mrs. Bloom always insisted I stay for dinner. My uncle—he was raising me after Dad died—he'd allow it, but under protest. *(Shrugs.)* They were Jews; he probably thought they'd try to circumcise me. Excuse me. One summer—I was ten—Mrs. Bloom asked me if I wanted to stay over. I said no, I didn't. I did want to, but I knew Uncle would say no. That's not true. I said no, because I wasn't sure how they slept. I knew it wasn't four to a room like me and my uncle and two of the Sunrise waiters, three snorers and me. But you don't say no to Mrs. Bloom. She went to the laundry and in front of everyone she told Uncle: "Lee's staying over; get his toothbrush."

(Addressing NEIL and Audience by now.) But, by eleven, she's having major regrets; she's yelling at us to shut up and then she comes to the room. Lights out. She goes over to Max and I see her shape in the dark, I see her lean over his bed for moment—she's murmuring something I can't hear. Then she comes to my bed. I'm terrified. Terrified, curious too—what is this crazy woman doing, this "mother" doing. And she does this: she pulls the covers up around me, she leans over and says something, not English, for sure not Cantonese. I'm pretending to be asleep, I feel her breath, and then she kisses my forehead. First kiss.

As soon as she's gone, Max wants to talk again, but I don't. I need to think. And this is what I thought. "This is what it's like. This must be what a mother does. This must be what happens in a family." And I swore, with all the ferocity a ten-year-old can muster: someday I will get this for myself.

(Back to SADIE.) Mrs. Bloom has cancer. Flowers are a stupid way to show how grateful I am. I'll help Max, I'll repay her that way—you—you are—crying—what are—

LEE reaches over and touches SADIE's cheek. He brushes away a tear. He tastes the tear. He touches her mouth. They kiss. SADIE eventually breaks off and exits.

NEIL: Are you OK?

LEE nods.

I didn't know any of that. I really am too naive to be a novelist. You and Mrs. Munro were—

LEE: We were in love. Two years. One month. Four days.

NEIL: *(More to himself.)* Lovers. But how?

LEE: How? Same as you and Christine. I climb on top, she closes her eyes and thinks of houses with no basements. Oh—how could she be in love with a "Chinaman"?

NEIL: You were her driver!

LEE: Yes—I was her "servant." What's that book they won't let through customs? The woman in it has sex with her gardener.

NEIL: They're English!

LEE: You mean, they're both English. *(Pause.)* But it's just not possible she killed me. I told you—I never saw her that morning—oh God, why can't I remember?—It *had* to be someone else.

CHRISTINE enters.

NEIL: Wait—she doesn't figure in this—

LEE: She's your fiancée.

NEIL: She hasn't been back since the funeral, six months ago.

LEE: Maybe she's got something to confess. *(Returns to his area.)*

CHRISTINE: Oh Neil, I'm sorry, I haven't been here since the funeral. I just couldn't. The lawsuit is starting; my lawyer thinks I have a good chance. And if I get to keep the money I'll give some to your old high school, like I promised. Maybe a quarter of it. Well, I have to go now. I'm working at Wilkie's Funeral Home. Mr. Bloom fired me, well, he's mad about the money. I had to quit teachers' college. Wilkie's nice. Sometimes he borrows my lipstick. Oh, shaving cream, look who's coming.

BLOOM arrives.

BLOOM: What are you doing here?

CHRISTINE: I'm visiting Neil. Why are you here?

BLOOM: I thought I'd dig up his stone and see if there's any money under it I can steal.

CHRISTINE: Ha ha.

CHRISTINE leaves. BLOOM goes to LEE's grave, perhaps putting a pebble on it.

BLOOM: I don't know what to do about your money, Lee. If I win the lawsuit I'll give it to charity, I guess. But that loan—who do I make the payments to? It doesn't seem right I should keep the money. After all, I caused your death. *(Leaves.)*

NEIL: Are you going to explain that for us?

LEE: No.

NEIL: You want me to speculate?

LEE: A couple of years ago I started the games at Max's. Wednesdays and Saturdays. Non-Chinese clientele. Max had nice chairs and tables to play on—it was classy. Maxie didn't have anything to do with the games; he just gave me a key and looked the other way.

NEIL: But why would he risk?—

LEE: He's not a businessman like his Dad. Max over-extended—that fancy house, the babies and then he tried stocking in all that sore-ass Danish stuff. No one was buying. The bank was going to foreclose. I lent him my profits. That forty-two thousand was a loan for next year's stock. Max was saved—and my problems were solved with the bank. I guess you could say Max was my Chinese money laundry.

NEIL: You know, if you're sure Mrs. Munro didn't kill you, maybe it was Bloom. He had a motive; he just said he "caused" your death, (whatever that means)

LEE: He was my brother.

BETTY swings in.

BETTY: Well, it wasn't me, either. Gimme a light, Chinaman.

NEIL: Mr. Kwan to you.

BETTY: And I'm Zig, daughter'a Zog. Now gimme a light; my trial's coming up and I'm gonna smoke for dramatic effect. *(On the stand.)* Your Honour, I feel real bad that my brother Terry—shanked—that reporter. But I'm not my brother's keeper. You see, Terry always was the rotten apple in the family barrel.

TERRY: *(Pauses while breaking rocks. To Audience.)* Nice sister, eh?

BETTY: No matter how much moral guidance I gave him.

TERRY reacts.

When he moved here he sent me a postcard of the cereal mill and said he was onta something big and I thought, Praise the Lord, he's got a real job, puffin' wheat. This I gotta see. But Terry wasn't puffin' any wheat. He was shanking guys in basements, which we know to be wrong in a civilized society.

CHIEF: Who's paying your lawyer?

BETTY: Never mind that.

CHIEF: Tell the court his name.

BETTY: It's irrelevent.

CHIEF: You're under oath.

BETTY: Heck Munro.

Community sound of horror.

Most decent fella I ever knew, by a long shot.

LAND's study.

SADIE: *(Holding up Gazette.)* "She met a fella." I can't believe Heck put this in his own paper.

LAND: In court she actually named him.

SADIE: How humiliating.

LAND: I'm only telling you that because I have some good news. He's going to cut her loose. They acquitted her and he's going over there this afternoon to end it.

SADIE: He told you he's ending it?

LAND: No, I'm telling him. He's stopping by in a few minutes.

LAND turns to face HECK.

HECK: I don't know if I can do that, Reverend. I love the woman.

LAND: *(Very tentatively.)* You'll end it, or burn in hell.

HECK: I beg your pardon?

LAND: Cut her loose—or burn in hell.

HECK: Did you just tell me?—I could have (sworn you said)

LAND: YOU'LL BURN IN HELL!

HECK: *(Backing out of office.)* I've never heard you talk like this—

LAND: YOU'LL BE CURSED! YOU'LL BE SHUNNED! CUT HER LOOSE OR NEVER DARKEN THIS CHURCH AGAIN! *(To Audience.)* Wow. Wow. My word. I don't know if any of you are clergy, but Lordy, you oughta give that a whirl. YOU'RE GONNA BURN! Whew. Phew. BURN! BURN!

LEE: *(To Audience.)* Makes me glad I'm Buddhist.

CHRISTINE storms on, followed by BETTY.

CHRISTINE: Let me say this one thing about the judicial process. Sure, you got acquitted as an accessory, but trust me, there is still a systemic bias against women.

LEE: Maxie won the lawsuit?

CHRISTINE: Of course Bloom won. *(As LEE celebrates.)* He's a man. And now, according to Canadian common law, finders are no longer keepers. *(To NEIL.)* You know, I shouldn't be surprised. You're telling the story. You're a man. A patronizing, paternalistic, pseudo-Hemingway. I'M SO GLAD WE NEVER GOT MARRIED! Come on, Betty.

NEIL: Actually, she has to stay.

CHRISTINE: Oh, right. You need her as an icon of the fallen woman. And Jean. Where's Jean? Jean, GET OVER HERE! Woman as bitch. There you have us. The unholy trinity. Slut, bitch, whore.

NEIL: Betty did something unexpected and incorrect—even for the 1950s. She stayed in her apartment and pined.

JEAN &
CHRISTINE: Pined?

BETTY: For Heck. Because he took Land's advice, and stayed away.

CHRISTINE: You are a gender traitor.

JEAN: I'd never pine for Archie.

BETTY: I eventually got wise.

NEIL: But this is all beside the point.

BETTY: What is the point?

NEIL: The point is, none of us ever really gave any serious thought to what happened to Lee here. As if he didn't matter. Like he was just some dead Chinaman lying under a car, and nothing more. But he's why we're stuck here. We should've left hours—days—ago, but we didn't, we can't, because we're all stuck and, and, well, we're stuck. Stuck. And so am I. Stuck.

CHIEF: Need rescuing, Scoop?

NEIL: Why—do you have any ideas?

CHIEF: It seems to me that we got a buncha people who plan on going to their graves with bits of information they should be giving to me while they're still alive—but aren't, for a variety of reasons. But once they're dead, they won't have any need to hide anything.

NEIL: So?

CHIEF: So, in other words, you're the writer—whyncha kill the buggers off?

NEIL: You're right! OK! You're all dead. Start talking!

General derisory rhubarb. NEIL turns back to CHIEF.

CHIEF: I kinda had something more writerly in mind.

NEIL: Oh. Of course. *(Thinks.)* I've got it. The Parade of Death. "The Parade of Death." How's that? Uh—who was first? *(Indicates BETTY.)* Ah, you, right. OK. It's 1960. Sunday. Church is ending. Reverend Land—wrap it up.

LAND: And in conclusion, my dear flock: KEEP IT IN YOUR PANTS! Go in peace.

NEIL: Post-church babble.

Rhubarb including:

LAND: I hear Wilkie's made you a partner.

CHRISTINE: "Wilkie and MacCosham."

WILKIE: We're going Polynesian!

NEIL: *(Ending rhubarb.)* And, Betty—

ARCHIE: Why's she here?

HECK: Time we pushed off.

BETTY: Hello, Heck. Good to see you again, after how long? A decade? Time flies when you're pining. *(To SADIE.)* Hiya.

HECK: Uh, this is my wife, Sadie.

BETTY: I know. Her photo was in your wallet. Heck: I'm leaving town. I'm sick of waiting for you to get up the balls to cross the street and make me a dishonest woman again. *(Holds out necklace to SADIE.)* Here, honey. By rights, this is yours. *(And the earrings.)* These too. Sorry I can't return the *South Pacific* tickets or that weekend at the Pierre. Or any of the sweat he left on me. *(Starting to leave.)* Reverend—just so you know: I don't regret a thing. The only thing better than sex before marriage—is sex during someone else's.

LAND: You'll rot in hell.

BETTY: I won't lack for company.

LAND: YOU SHALL BE STRUCK DOWN!

BETTY: *(To Audience.)* What am I thinking as I tip-tap across the front walk of First Presbyterian to the street? "You gave it to 'em good, Betty. And now, if you can just cross Water without tripping, you can let yourself have a good cry." *(Betty steps off the curb and looks south.)*

NEIL: Now, at this point you need to know that Water Street had been just made one-way—north. Betty got to the curb and quite naturally just looked one way—south. But Avery Tedford Junior was coming to town. Avery Junior had inherited his daddy's rock farm north of the city and he came here to put flowers on his father's grave once a year. How was Avery to know that Water now ran north only? He barrelled south…

A terrible thump.

SADIE: *(Running over.)* Oh my God!

HECK: Someone call an ambulance.

LAND: Could I have done that?

WILKIE and CHRISTINE are fussing over BETTY.

Is it possible I can literally cause people to be struck down?

HECK: It would appear so.

LAND: I was only preaching metaphorically. It's back to benevolence for me. *(To WILKIE.)* We want to do the right thing by her.

HECK: No expenses spared.

WILKIE: I doubt I can do a thing for her right side.

HECK: Why not have a closed casket?

WILKIE: Why not throw her in the river and let her float to Zion?

HECK: But nothing South Pacific, Wilkie. No burning pigs. Nothing Buddhist—

WILKIE: Do I tell you what typeface to use? Now shoo. We've got work to do, a lot of it.

LAND and HECK leave. BETTY turns to NEIL and talks, as WILKIE and CHRISTINE put finishing touches to her. They eventually move off.

NEIL: Was it your brother who killed Lee?

BETTY: Of course it was Terry.

TERRY: *(Pauses while breaking rocks.)* What!

LEE: He told you he did it?

BETTY: Not in so many words, but you don't have to be Einstein to connect Terry's ugly dots. But he was too stupid to act on his own.

BETTY moves off.

NEIL: So she thinks—

CHIEF: He always denied killing him.

TERRY: Hardly laid a finger on him.

Centennial music begins, under.

NEIL: *(To CHIEF.)* That's your cue. Ashburnham's Centennial Parade! *(To Audience.)* Let's watch for the final car—the Chief's. He's retiring this year, so they gave him the honour.

CHIEF: Forty years a cop and only one unsolved case. *(Clutches chest.)* Oh oh.

NEIL: The coroner will say heart attack.

CHIEF: That damn fool always says heart attack. *(Grabs chest.)* But yup, he might be right this time.

LEE: Bad timing—smack in the middle of the Humiliation Day parade!

NEIL: *(Forgetting about CHIEF.)* Humiliation Day?

LEE: An Act Respecting the Immigration of "Chinamen."

NEIL: Right, right—

LEE: The Exclusion Act of 1923. July 1. Humiliation Day.

NEIL: Yeah, well, for most of us, it's Dominion Day and this year it happens to be the hundredth anniversary of Confederation.

LEE: You say Confederation, I say Humiliation.

NEIL: This is that brief shining moment in our collective history when there's a massive outpouring of, of—

LEE: Denial.

CHIEF: Oh, dry up and let me die in peace. *(Dies.)*

WILKIE and CHRISTINE tear back on.

WILKIE: Such a big man. His face'll use up an entire pot of foundation, I predict.

Coughing from HECK.

And I also predict we'll be having a deluxe Heck Munro funeral soon.

WILKIE and CHRISTINE turn their attention to HECK.

HECK: *(Lights a cigarette, turns to Audience.)* Yes, yes, they did kill me—but not until late August of 1970, thank God. Because there was one more editorial I had to write, one more chance for me to get the people of this city—all one hundred thousand of them—if you count those bizarre new suburbs to our south—to go beyond received wisdom and actually think. So here goes. "On this, the 25th anniversary of the Hiroshima bombing, I pose this question to you, my dear readers. What's the difference between the Holocaust in Europe and our atom bombing of Hiroshima? Answer: The Germans apologized."

JEAN: "The Germans apologized"! He's lost his marbles!

ARCHIE: What exactly is he saying—we were wrong to end the war?

JEAN: Poor Sadie. What she's been through.

CHRISTINE: Imagine writing such a thing!

LAND: Heck's right. I know only too well the evil of striking people down. I'm going to stick up for him this Sunday.

NEIL: But you never made it.

CHRISTINE: They're dropping like flies!

WILKIE: Excellent!

They go to work on LAND.

LAND: And I was, in fact, next. Oh—nothing dramatic. In my sleep. I was dreaming about Jericho, oddly enough. The walls tumbling down. Well, there were some nymphs, too. But mostly it was walls. And then there was a deep voice, speaking in a light Scottish burr. Just the voice you'd expect God to have. But it wasn't God at all. It was Sean Connery.

WILKIE and CHRISTINE escort BLOOM on.

BLOOM: I died on the eighteenth hole of The Blue Monster at Doral. I'd faded my second shot over the water and landed on the green—I could've birdied. That's as close to paradise on earth as any golfer's going to get, so I went, right then. My sons brought me home. Wilkie drove the hearse down Water, past the old store. It's a bingo hall now. So listen, Lee, right about now the boys are having a little read of my will—

JEAN: I just saw on the six o'clock news—

CHRISTINE: That blankety-blank man left forty-two thousand dollars—

WILKIE: For a statue commemorating the what Act?

LEE: The Exclusion Act!

JEAN: You want exclusion! We're so poor we're excluded from even having a front lawn.

BLOOM: My idea is to have a group of Chinese men on one side of the street—men like your Dad and your uncle—and they're reaching across Water towards a group of women—who have no faces.

CHRISTINE: And he's left land for the statue—

WILKIE: An old Fina station.

ARCHIE: Our old front yard!

JEAN: And he paid for it with my money!

There is a major crash of bulldozers. Sound of stones falling. It stops. SADIE hustles on.

LEE: I don't think you'll get to finish the story. Nobody's coming through with a confession.

NEIL: Who's left alive?

SADIE: Me, Christine—Wilkie, Terry Andrews, the Copelands—

NEIL: Archie and Jean first.

ARCHIE is standing atop a highrise. JEAN and CHRISTINE and WILKIE are trying to talk him down.

JEAN: Arch, grow up!

ARCHIE: This is what you've always wanted.

JEAN: I only wanted it when I knew you were too chicken-livered to do it.

ARCHIE: I'm not chicken now! Finally this city's got a building high enough to jump from. Sixty years I've waited for this. And it's a Senior Citizens' residence—how fitting. Jean, I'm finally making you a happy woman!

JEAN: It's way too late for that.

ARCHIE: I'm jumping and I'm taking my secret with me. I know who murdered Lee Kwan!

CHRISTINE: Mr. Bloom's friend—

ARCHIE: The Munros' chauffeur.

WILKIE: My epiphany.

ARCHIE: He was murdered three days before your Neil. That money you found was his!

CHRISTINE: It wasn't Bloom's?

JEAN: This was fifty years ago!

ARCHIE: So.

JEAN: Well, as if anyone cares.

CHRISTINE: I do!

ARCHIE: See. Oh, you'd care too, Jean. You'd be shocked beyond belief.

JEAN: Then shock me, Arch. Tell us who killed Lee Kwan.

WILKIE: Everyone knows it was Heck Munro. He killed him because he found out Lee was having an affair with Sadie.

The other three turn in surprise.

JEAN: What?

CHRISTINE: —What?

ARCHIE: —What!

ARCHIE loses his balance and falls. CHRISTINE, WILKIE and JEAN rush to the edge and look. Reverend LAND greets ARCHIE and dusts him off.

LAND: Welcome, my child. It's a land of milk and honey.

ARCHIE: Any poker?

LAND: No. No cards.

ARCHIE: Nuts.

ARCHIE shuffles back. Lies down. Life support beeping begins.

JEAN: *(To Audience.)* He'll be on life support forever, I just know it! Well, I won't stand for it. *(To ARCHIE.)* Arch. You have to take a hike. *(Tender.)* Goodbye, you old fool.

JEAN disconnects ARCHIE from life support. Long beep. ARCHIE stands up and begins to shuffle towards the others again. He stops.

ARCHIE: Absolutely no poker?

LAND: Sorry.

Everyone shakes their heads. ARCHIE tries to return to life support and is met by JEAN, pointing him back to the dead.

JEAN: NO!

ARCHIE: Then come with me. *(Holds out his hand.)*

JEAN: I have to close up the house, I have to make sure they move the family crypt to that place by the freeway—why should I?

ARCHIE: Nobody on the other side knows the Archie you married.

JEAN: *(Beat.)* True, there's just me.

ARCHIE: That's all there's ever been.

JEAN: Well, that, and poker. OK, Arch. OK. You win.

WILKIE and CHRISTINE arrive, dead.

WILKIE: You wouldn't like it back there. Even funerals are changing. People drive their dead to the south end—there's a warehouse where they do it all cheap. You drop your loved one off and an hour later she comes back out, dressed, stuffed, boxed—have a nice day, honey.

CHRISTINE: *(Rattling pills.)* So I decided to come with him.

JEAN and ARCHIE join the dead. TERRY enters.

TERRY: Hiya, sis.

BETTY: Took you long enough to get here. I've been bored out of my gourd.

TERRY kisses her on the cheek.

What's that for?

TERRY: I dunno. I'm glad to see ya. I haven't kissed a woman in fifty years. And don't worry. I'm a new man. You won't believe what prison's done for me. I got my B.A. in Philosophy, my Master's in Abnormal Psychology and a week before I died I got my Ph.D. in Early Childhood Education.

BETTY: That's good, 'cause it's all pretty civilized here.

CHIEF: And it's time for you to relax your Felon's Code of Ethics and tell us who murdered Lee Kwan.

TERRY: No way. I may be educated, but I'm still a con.

SADIE enters.

SADIE: Hurry! I can't hold them off any longer!

They all look at NEIL.

NEIL: I, uh—none of you—no one revealed (anything)

LEE: So much for the Parade of Death.

NEIL: Sir? Help?

CHIEF: We'll, uh, we'll try something else. A re-enactment. See if we missed something along the way.

NEIL: But that's how I started!

CHIEF: You got fancy and left stuff out. Went on a little—what'd he call it?

HECK: A road trip to the truth.

CHIEF: And you got sidetracked.

SADIE: Does nobody care that I confessed?

NEIL: It's just that we don't believe you—

SADIE: Oh for God's sakes! I'll prove it. *(To Audience.)* It's 1949. June. The sun is peeking over Ludgate Hill. You've heard the town's alarm clocks and he apologized for them. *(To the dead.)* I'm re-enacting! Move! It's 7:00 A.M. Heck? Where are you? Heck! Heck! I want the car today—Lee and I are going to the lake and—

Sound of door slamming offstage.

Damn you. Damn you. *(To HECK.)* Go!

HECK: I'm in the garage. *(To LEE.)* On the fritz again? I'm going to buy you a Caddy, Lee. I swear it. OK?

LEE: I don't remember any of this.

CHIEF: None of it?

LEE: No.

NEIL: *(To BLOOM.)* Bloom—you're next. Over at your store.

BLOOM: Oh—my head.

CHIEF: But it's not a hangover, is it?

BLOOM: Sheesh. What's this—phew! What is that smell?

CHIEF: Let me guess—you can't remember either?

BLOOM nods.

(Sotto.) I've got it!

Telephone rings at MUNRO house. Everyone looks at it.

SADIE: *(To LAND.)* Time to open your big mouth. *(Picks up phone.)* Riverside 20189.

LAND: Sadie—it's Wilf Land.

SADIE: This is early, Reverend. Has someone died? I'm going up north to get some flowers—I can get you some.

LAND: No, no, nothing like that Sadie. I've had a—a request. *(To NEIL.)* May I?

NEIL: Yes.

LAND: You're not going to stop me in the name of dramatic structure?

NEIL and SADIE motion for him to hurry.

Your driver came to me yesterday. He's asked me to intervene in an immigration matter. He's bringing over a young woman from China and he wants me as sponsor. It's odd—he asked me not to speak to Heck or you about it. Should I go ahead?

SADIE: With—

LAND: With helping him bring this woman here.

SADIE: But I don't understand—is it a sister? He never mentioned one.

LAND: No, he says it's his fiancée.

SADIE: His what?

LAND: Fiancée. From his ancestral village. An arranged thing, I believe. We have to make speed with this, he says, because of the political situation there. When the Communists take over, it may not be possible to get people out.

SADIE: Fiancée?

LAND: Do I have your consent to proceed? Sadie—are you still there. Sadie?

SADIE: Yes. Of course. Yes. Full steam ahead.

SADIE puts her phone down. And then she puts her face in her hands, and gives herself over to anger and grief. The others are embarrassed. SADIE looks up, finally.

He had been sleeping with me for two years, both of us risking everything—and all this time he's planning to bring some woman over from China! Someone he's never even met! I went down to the garage. Calling for him. My thirty-nine years of "energetically sad" giving way to "Come out of there!" But he was too goddamn cowardly to come out, so I began hitting him. I had the tire iron and I hit him, on the head, and—and then, well, there was no sound, so I pulled on the tarp, I dragged him out—he was dead.

The CHIEF is shaking his head.

What?

CHIEF: May I?

NEIL: Be my guest.

CHIEF: You see, that morning back in 1949 started a bit earlier than you realize. In fact, it started before our friend Max here woke up on his Danish chair. Archie?

JEAN: What's Archie got to do with anything?—

ARCHIE: It's OK. Sadie, you didn't kill Lee. I did.

Rhubarb.

JEAN: That's the (most ridiculous thing)

HECK: Oh for God's sake, Chief, Kid—Sadie's confessed. For that matter, Betty's implicated Terry, Bloom's taking the blame, how many murderers do you need? We have to get the hell out of here.

CHIEF: Not so fast, Munro.

NEIL: You're not the editor anymore. Sir.

CHIEF: I've noticed something about you. You're so used to having the soapbox all to yourself it isn't necessary for you to listen to anyone. For example—when you came down to see Lee that morning—at what, 7:00?—I have a hunch Lee wasn't even alive. And if he wasn't alive at 7:00 then your wife certainly didn't kill him at 8:30. No, I think we've got to go back earlier that day—how early, Arch?

ARCHIE: 5:30.

JEAN: Archie—no!

ARCHIE: Just before dawn.

CHIEF: And it all starts with the money Lee was hiding away in that wall, doesn't it? Terry?

TERRY looks innocent.

ARCHIE: You were there, too.

TERRY: There's a name for guys like you. Stoolpigeon.

They go into the real re-enactment.

BLOOM: I actually wasn't at the store overnight. I'd gone in really early, to do inventory. *(Sees TERRY.)* How'd you get in here?

TERRY: Where's the money?

BLOOM: What money?

TERRY: *(Pulling knife.)* It's here somewhere.

BLOOM: Everything goes to the night deposit.

TERRY: From the gambling.

BLOOM: I don't know what you're talking about.

TERRY: Where is it! Listen pal, you got kids? You better talk.

BLOOM: There's the float. You can have it—

TERRY roughs him up a bit.

OK, OK, he keeps stuff in the basement. I don't know where. *(As TERRY threatens more.)* Far wall. Beside the fuse box. There's a brick, pull it out—

TERRY nods to ARCHIE, who is wearing a balaclava. He steps out behind BLOOM and chloroforms him while TERRY holds him. BLOOM struggles, then collapses. TERRY accidentally gets a whiff and buckles too.

TERRY: Careful, that stuff's powerful.

He pushes BLOOM over to the couch.

ARCHIE: *(Takes off balaclava.)* These things itch! I hope he's OK. I didn't know how much to use.

TERRY: Aw, he'll wake up with a headache—

ARCHIE: *(Over.)* He's a nice man. Gosh, should we prop him up? Is he still breathing? Will he be OK?

TERRY: Leave him! Come on!

Basement. Stage goes to black. Two flashlights.

ARCHIE: Why don't the lights work?

TERRY: How the hell would I know?

ARCHIE: How can you tell which wall is the far one?

TERRY: Quit asking questions!

ARCHIE: What if he was lying to us? Sorry, (sorry)

TERRY: OK, here's the fusebox. Hold on—OK, brick—Jesus—there's nothing here. I'll kill that Jew! Someone's moved the box. Wait—he said—that's it—it's gotta be the Chink.

ARCHIE: Why?—

TERRY: He runs the games. Where's he live?

ARCHIE: Oh, ah, well—

TERRY: You're in this, you're in it as deep as me. You want your money back? Where's he live!

ARCHIE: He's Heck Munro's driver. He lives up Water Street—where are you going?

TERRY: Where do you think? Come on.

ARCHIE: Should I bring the mask?

TERRY: Yeah, that'd be real subtle. Let's walk up Water Street wearing masks. Jesus, you're a dolt.

LEE comes to garage and flicks light on.

LEE: This is a little embarrassing, but I had begun talking to the car. Well, it did have a personality. So, Mr. Packard, you will start this morning, won't you?

Sound of car not starting.

Mr. Munro wants to visit his girl before work and he wants as much time as he can and if you don't start he'll have to walk and—

Car still isn't starting. LEE swears in Cantonese.

It's the damn electrical.

LEE spreads out the tarp and takes off his jacket.

Now, Mr. Packard. You see that I am ready to go under you and tickle your belly and get myself all dirty and ruin my day. You've made your point. So why don't you be kind to me, your humble servant, your best buddy—start this time—

Car starts. Purrs under.

Ah, my lucky day!

LEE starts cleaning the car. There's a noise. He turns and listens. Another noise.

Mr. Munro? Sir?

No answer. But LEE knows he's heard something. He turns car off.

Mr. Munro?

TERRY appears, with knife.

Why are you here?

TERRY: Whaddya think?

LEE: You get out.

TERRY: Give me the money.

LEE: What money?—I'll call for help—

TERRY: You've got it here.

LEE: I don't know what you're talking about—

TERRY: Don't play dumb—

LEE: The money's in Bloom's basement—

TERRY lunges at LEE and they start fighting. LEE manages to kick the knife from TERRY's hand and looks like he's starting to get the upper hand, when ARCHIE steps out from behind the wall. He grabs LEE from behind—and chloroforms him. LEE struggles a lot more than BLOOM; ARCHIE must keep the rag over his face until LEE collapses—and even then ARCHIE can't or won't release his grip. LEE slides to the floor. ARCHIE and TERRY stand over him, panting.

TERRY: OK, let's find the box.

TERRY and ARCHIE tear around looking for it.

ARCHIE: It's probably in his room.

TERRY: Maybe. Wait a second—that tarp—he's been under the car—

ARCHIE: You don't think it's under there—

TERRY: Why not?—it'd be the perfect spot—

TERRY gets on the tarp and slides under the car. The door slams, offstage.

HECK: *(Off.)* Lee! Lee?

ARCHIE: It's Heck!

ARCHIE pushes LEE behind the car and hides. TERRY slides beneath the car but doesn't manage to get all the way under; his legs are sticking out as at the top of the play.

HECK: *(Coming on; sees "LEE's" feet under car.)* On the fritz again? OK, I'm going to walk to work. *(Going off.)* I promise, Lee, I'll get you a Caddy. You'd like that, eh?

HECK has gone. The lights begin dimming on TERRY, ARCHIE and LEE—and a tight spot grows on NEIL. He has his notepad out, and is jotting down details as events unfold behind him.

TERRY: Is he gone?

ARCHIE is groaning. TERRY slides out.

What's your problem?

ARCHIE: It's Lee. He's not—he's—he's not breathing—he's—he's dead—

TERRY: That's ridiculous.

TERRY slaps LEE once or twice.

You musta overdid the chemicals. Let's get the hell outa here.

ARCHIE: But we can't leave him—

TERRY: Yeah, let's drag him down Water. Jesus. OK—what to do?—We gotta buy some time—Let's hide him—OK—Help me with him.

ARCHIE: What're you doing?—

TERRY: Shove. SHOVE!

TERRY is pushing LEE under the car.

ARCHIE: But we have to—

TERRY: What?

ARCHIE: Shouldn't we phone a doctor?

TERRY: What's that gonna prove? Hey—look—he's working on the car. OK, let's get the hell out of here—

ARCHIE: Where!

TERRY: I don't know. The Coffee Shop. You go home.

TERRY and ARCHIE exit.

NEIL: And Arch went to the bridge—and didn't jump. And you came down in a rage—and didn't kill him. And—and now we can leave.

Massive lights on everyone. The bulldozers are virtually upon them.

Is everyone ready?

General assent.

Any last words?

HECK: We've got all of eternity for that, Kid.

NEIL: I mean—to them. They're leaving in five minutes.

The group turns to survey the Audience.

WILKIE: Wait—they aren't coming with us?

NEIL: Not if they can help it. So—anyone? Anything?

A pause.

TERRY: I got something. If you ever go to jail for murder, do your time constructively.

NEIL: Oohh kay.

BETTY: *(A shrug.)* Live your life like you're crossing Water—always look both ways.

NEIL: That's nice.

BETTY and TERRY are leaving.

CHRISTINE: If you ever hit the jackpot—keep it to yourself.

LAND: Hellfire and damnation is cheap trickery. All you need is love.

NEIL: That's not original.

LAND: It's from the Bible.

NEIL: Oh.

WILKIE: I have an important one. If you're afraid of something, look deep into that fear, find the most important thing about it—and make it your life's work.

WILKIE, LAND and CHRISTINE are leaving.

ARCHIE: *(As he gets to LEE.)* I'm sorry. I didn't mean to—

LEE accepts his apology. JEAN turns to BLOOM.

JEAN: A lifetime being ashamed—isn't better.

BLOOM: *(Accepts this, then:)* Life *is* better—without a basement.

CHIEF: Start your day with a full breakfast!

BLOOM, CHIEF, JEAN and ARCHIE leave. HECK is looking out at SADIE.

NEIL: Sir?

HECK: I, uh—you coming, Sadie?

NEIL: She can't. She's not one of us yet.

HECK: I'll be waiting for you. *(To Audience.)* I'm right about Hiroshima.

HECK leaves.

NEIL: So that's that. I hope you'll visit us in our new resting place. I believe they're calling it The Pioneer Memorial. They're arranging us along the right bank of the freeway, formerly Water; wave at us as you barrel south. Um, drive home carefully. Make sure you didn't drop anything under your seat; the theatre doesn't need any more umbrellas. Jeez. Now that it's time to leave, I don't want to. Lee. Come on.

LEE: Not without her.

NEIL: She has to go home with them.

LEE: We'll be along soon.

NEIL: But I don't know if it's possible for me to go and have the story continue—

LEE: Give it a try. If you're truly a great writer you should be able to disappear—and the world you created will live on. For a minute or two, at least.

NEIL: Oh. Well.

LEE: Try.

NEIL: OK. *(To Audience.)* OK. This is Neil Griffin. Your sometime-omniscient narrator. Signing off.

NEIL snaps his fingers and the light goes out on him. From the darkness:

It worked!

Only LEE and SADIE are lit.

LEE: The first time I understood belonging was the night Mrs. Bloom kissed me goodnight. The second time I understood was there, on your island, on those rocks, your flowers at our feet, our feet surrounded by water, the same water that aches to join the river, the same river that is dying to flow as far away from us as fast as it can. The second time I belonged happened because I was able to tell you about that first time. *(To Audience.)* And because you understand my story, we are free to start a new one.

SADIE has closed her eyes during this. LEE gently opens them. She has died. They exit.

Black.

The End

Acknowledgments

The creation of this play was inspired by Thornton Wilder's *Our Town*.

Walking on Water was commissioned by Prairie Theatre Exchange and The Grand Theatre (London, Ontario). It was developed with assistance from The Canadian Stage Company and the National Arts Centre, the Canada Council and the Ontario Arts Council.

In addition to the actors directly involved in the productions of this play, a great number have also participated in the development of the script. They include Denis Akiyama, Nancy Beatty, David Bolt, Pierre Brault, George Chiang, Jerry Doyle, Todd Duckworth, Peter Duschenes, Paul Essiembre, David Fox, Susan Glover, Peter Froehlich, Henry Gauthier, Graham Harley, Kate Hemblen, Fiona Highet, John Jarvis, Jason Jazrawy, Maureen Kirkpatrick, John Koensgen, Jeff Lawson, Richard MacMillan, John Ng, Nancy Palk, Alex Poch-Goldin, Paul Rainville, Shannon Reynolds, Rick Roberts, Alison Sealy-Smith, Dixie Seatle, Greg Spottiswood, Aron Tager, Maria Vacratsis, Sarah van Diepen, Michael Waller and Beverley Wolfe.

Dramaturgical advice: Candace Burley, Margaret Carley, Lise Anne Johnson, Katharine Kaszas, Bill Lane, Joan McRae, Alicia Perry, Betty Quan, Randy Read, James Roy, Michael Shamata and, especially, Iris Turcott.

My particular thanks go to the two directors of *Walking on Water*, both of whom had a vast (and benign) influence on the play's development: Allen MacInnes and Michael Waller.

About the Author

Dave Carley is the author of a number of works for stage, including *Writing With Our Feet, After You, A View From The Roof, Taking Liberties* and, most recently, a dramatization of Margaret Atwood's novel *The Edible Woman*. He has been nominated for the Governor General's Award for Drama and is a three-time Chalmers Award finalist. He received the 2000 Arthur Miller Playwriting Award from the University of Michigan and has been the playwright-in-residence at Ontario's Stratford Festival and Barrington Stage Company in Massachusetts. Dave was born and raised in Peterborough, Ontario, and currently lives in Toronto.